These
Valiant
Dead

Renewing
the Past in
Shakespeare's
Histories

Robert C. Jones

These
Valiant
Dead

University of Iowa Press

Iowa City

University of Iowa Press,
Iowa City 52242
Copyright © 1991 by
the University of Iowa
All rights reserved
Printed in the
United States of America
First edition, 1991

Design by Richard Hendel

Printed on acid-free paper

Library of Congress Cataloging-in-Publication Data
Jones, Robert C., 1936–
    These valiant dead: renewing the past in Shakespeare's
histories / by Robert C. Jones.—1st ed.
    p.   cm.
    Includes bibliographical references and index.
    ISBN 0-87745-308-X (alk. paper)
    1. Shakespeare, William, 1564–1616—Histories.
2. Great Britain—History—1066–1687—Historiography.
3. Historical drama, English—History and criticism.
4. Kings and rulers in literature.   5. Great Britain in
literature.   6. Heroes in literature.   I. Title.
PR2982.J66   1991   90-46586
822.3′3—dc20   CIP

To Kathy

CONTENTS

Introduction

Behind the turbulent action of Shakespeare's histories stands a figure who is often called upon by the embattled characters onstage to place their current problems in the perspective he affords them—and, of course, to offer us the advantage of that perspective as well. From the dead march that signals the opening of *1 Henry VI* to the Chorus's closing lines at the end of *Henry V*, the image of the lost leader is evoked time and again to set and characterize the present scene by those who remember him and feel his loss. As we in the audience look "back" at the historical figures onstage, they look back at him, and our perspective on them deepens through their own recollections. Sometimes the remembered hero—a Henry V, or a Hotspur—is one who struts

or frets onstage himself in the course of the histories. But others—
the Black Prince, Edward III, Richard Cordelion—who never actually appear in person serve as significant presences when they
are recalled by those who do.

I have begun by calling this remembered hero a lost leader, but
in this case there is a great deal in a name. I want to strip away
from this one the clouds of infamy that it comes trailing from
Browning's poem. The former leader evoked in these plays is lost
to the present because he is dead, because he now belongs to the
past, not because he has turned his coat or betrayed his cause. But
to say that he is lost to the present *does* suggest the negative, or
his negation, and its impact on a world that feels diminished (or
threatened, or ruined) by his passing:

> Hung be the heavens with black, yield day to night!
> Comets, importing change of times and states,
> Brandish your crystal tresses in the sky
> And with them scourge the bad revolting stars
> That have consented unto Henry's death—
> King Henry the Fifth, too famous to live long!
> England ne'er lost a king of so much worth.
>
>   (*1HVI*, I, i, 1–7)[1]

This, however, is only one side of the story. Though such a loss
and its consequences are frequently the burden of remembrance,
there is also a positive potential in the memory of the past leader
that belies the very notion that he is lost. Consider the opposite
impulses of the following recollections of the Black Prince, both
addressed to young monarchs by their elder counsellors:

> I am the last of noble Edward's sons,
> Of whom thy father, Prince of Wales, was first.
> In war was never lion raged more fierce,
> In peace was never gentle lamb more mild,
> Than was that young and princely gentleman.

His face thou hast, for even so looked he,
Accomplished with the number of thy hours;
But when he frowned, it was against the French
And not against his friends. His noble hand
Did win what he did spend, and spent not that
Which his triumphant father's hand had won.
His hands were guilty of no kinred blood,
But bloody with the enemies of his kin.
O Richard! York is too far gone with grief,
Or else he never would compare between.

(*RII*, II, i, 171–185)

Gracious lord,
Stand for your own, unwind your bloody flag,
Look back into your mighty ancestors;
Go, my dread lord, to your great-grandsire's tomb,
From whom you claim; invoke his warlike spirit,
And your great-uncle's, Edward the Black Prince,
Who on the French ground played a tragedy,
Making defeat on the full power of France,
Whiles his most mighty father on a hill
Stood smiling to behold his lion's whelp
Forage in blood of French nobility.
O noble English, that could entertain
With half their forces the full pride of France
And let another half stand laughing by,
All out of work and cold for action!

(*HV*, I, ii, 100–114)

And note the contrasting implications of the early lament for
Henry V and the later exhortation to him (which follows directly
on the lines just cited):

Henry is dead and never shall revive.
Upon a wooden coffin we attend,
And death's dishonorable victory

We with our stately presence glorify,
Like captives bound to a triumphant car.

.   .   .   .

Arms avail not, now that Henry's dead.
Posterity, await for wretched years,
When at their mothers' moist'ned eyes babes shall suck,
Our isle be made a nourish of salt tears,
And none but women left to wail the dead.

(*1HVI*, I, i, 18–51)

Awake remembrance of these valiant dead,
And with your puissant arm renew their feats.
You are their heir; you sit upon their throne;
The blood and courage that renownèd them
Runs in your veins; and my thrice-puissant liege
Is in the very May-morn of his youth,
Ripe for exploits and mighty enterprises.

(*HV*, I, ii, 115–121)

When he serves as a shining contrast to the dismal present, the dead leader seems "lost" indeed. But when he serves to inspire a present leader to "renew" his feats, and when remembrance of the "valiant dead" is thus awakened by (as it also awakens) a heroic action under way, then he does not belong only to the past, nor is he "lost" at all, but becomes "that ever-living man of memory" (*1HVI*, IV, iii, 51) whose vitalizing spirit still flourishes in the present. And as the evoked image shifts from the negative to the positive, from lost leader to inspirational model, the implied relationship between past and present shifts accordingly.

The full implications of the speeches cited above depend, of course, on their particular contexts. Our understanding of them includes our understanding of the situation (a funeral calls for a different retrospective tone than a council of war) and of the speaker (we will weigh the archbishop of Canterbury's exhortation to Henry V by his already revealed motives). Still, in their

fuller contexts, these recollections of the valiant dead are significant expressions of the sense of the past and its importance to the
present. However we place them, doing so involves us in exam-
ining the views of history and its uses that are dramatized in the
histories themselves. My primary focus on the varying images and
functions of the remembered dead hero, therefore, naturally extends out toward this larger topic of the developing ways in which
history is conceived through Shakespeare's nine plays about medieval England. And though I make no claim to explicate this larger
topic fully or finally, approaching it through the plays' own dramatized remembrances of the valiant dead offers instructive insights
into it. My primary concern here will be to trace the possibilities,
as they are suggested through the histories, for crediting a vital
relationship between past and present in which the valiant dead
can be renewed to benefit their successors.

This conception of history's value, as Shakespeare has Henry V's
counsellors articulate it, had for his time all the shiny simplicity
of a well-worn commonplace. Froissart had begun his account of
Henry's great-grandsire's times by committing himself to just such
an "awakening" as the informing purpose of his enterprise:

> To thentent that the honorable and noble aventures of
> featis of armes, done and achyved by the warres of France
> and Inglande, shulde notably be inregistered, and put in
> perpetual memory, whereby the prewe and hardy may have
> ensample to incourage them in theyr well doyng, I syr
> John Froissart, wyll treat and recorde an hystory of great
> lovage and preyse.[2]

When E. M. W. Tillyard reviewed "the chief ends of history for
the Elizabethans," his illustrative citations show that for writers as
otherwise diverse as Froissart's translator Berners, Tito Livio, and
Sir Walter Raleigh, the insistence on emulation of glorious predecessors took obvious precedence over the more particular lesson
about preservation of order that Tillyard himself was concerned

to emphasize.[3] And when Thomas Nashe applied the idea to plays (and illustrated it with the first in Shakespeare's own series of history plays), his very terms anticipate those in which Ely will urge Henry to renew the valiant dead and their feats:

> Nay, what if I proove Playes to be . . . a rare exercise of vertue? First, for the subiect of them (for the most part) it is borrowed out of our English Chronicles, wherein our forefathers valiant acts (that have line long buried in rustie brasse and worme-eaten bookes) are revived, and they themselves raised from the Grave of Oblivion, and brought to pleade their aged Honours in open presence.[4]

The idea of heroic emulation had coexisted with other more sober and pragmatic rationales for history and its uses, of course. And the "historical revolution" of Shakespeare's time, of which we are still the heirs, rendered such a lofty purpose at least doubly suspect.[5] When, for example, Bacon declared us much beholden to Machiavelli and others who tell us what men do rather than what they ought to do, he fired two deflating shots at the airy idealism of heroical history. One announced the consistent Baconian preference for the pragmatically useful over the imaginatively wishful—a preference that has been honored by respectable historical endeavors as well as other advancements of learning since his time. The other, implicit in the first, accuses any such glowing account of human behavior as Froissart promises and gives us of being "mere" fiction and therefore useless (or worse, dangerous).

Modern skepticism has improved on Bacon's deflation of false idols by calling into question the newer methods and surer results he so firmly advocated, and not least where history is concerned. Against his more pragmatic understanding and therefore presumably more useful application of history, one might set Paul Valéry's annihilating blast: "History is the most dangerous product evolved from the chemistry of the intellect. . . . It teaches precisely nothing, for it contains everything and furnishes examples of everything."[6] More subversive still to the absolute Baconian preference for truth over fiction is the awareness that accounts of what men have *done*, and not only what they *ought* to have done, are also fictively shaped to suit the historian's agenda and perspective.[7]

On all such matters, not surprisingly, Shakespeare was both of his age and beyond its more single-minded declarations. His history plays' counterpointed dialogue includes, along with heady exhortations to heroic emulation of the valiant dead, cool-headed analyses of what has been (and prognoses of what will be) done in the Machiavellian vein preferred by Bacon. And also included is the awareness that such pragmatic accounts of what is past or passing or to come may themselves be false conceptions or fictive constructions.

Much of the best recent thinking about the sense of history in Shakespeare's histories highlights this awareness of its fictive dimension.[8] Again, this is scarcely surprising at a time when all historical discourse, and not only historical fiction, has been subjected to the scrutiny of current theories about language and narrative. In such a critical climate, a study that begins as mine does by taking the idea of heroical history—already well worn by the time Shakespeare first dramatized it—pretty much at face value, as though Nashe could have been essentially right about the spirit he attributed to *1 Henry VI*, may seem to simplify its subject. I believe, however, that too deconstructive a reading of *1 Henry VI* can blur real and significant distinctions between that play (or the first tetralogy) and *Henry V* (or the second).[9] In any case, my argument inevitably does follow certain larger trends in thinking about Shakespeare's histories. While he was still engaged in breaking Tillyard's hold over these plays, Robert Ornstein was naturally interested in stressing the "personalism" evident in them—the fact that they, too, are concerned with human beings and human behavior and are not confined to illustrating a theory of history or supporting a political doctrine. He and others also challenged the view of history Tillyard ascribed to the plays.[10] In the wake of such endeavors, subsequent readers have focused on the plays' historical concerns in different ways, without either subscribing to Tillyard's authority or feeling obliged to do battle with it. My way will be to examine the conceptions of history expressed by characters in the plays themselves, together with their uses and abuses of their own historical understanding (or misunderstanding), and to infer whatever sense of history Shakespeare may offer us from such an examination.

Even within its methodological limits, the view offered here is not a comprehensive one. Though it is necessary to consider other kinds of retrospection in order to place and discuss remembrance of the valiant dead, my focus is on the latter. Since that focus is maintained throughout, the chapters do not pretend to be full interpretive readings of each individual play. On the other hand, I attempt to maintain a proper regard for each play as a play in its own right and to avoid treating them merely as parts of an essay on history unfolding toward its conclusion in *Henry V*. It has been argued, I believe correctly, that the history plays are inherently insusceptible to "conclusions" and that much of their generic distinctiveness from the other kinds of plays that Shakespeare wrote may be identified with this inconclusiveness.[11] I may bend the terms of that argument somewhat to make my point here, but inconclusiveness as aptly describes ideas about history articulated through these plays as it does their dramatic form.

Still, there is a difference between a form that calls attention to its inconclusiveness and an absence of any form at all. And though the plays' dramatization of varying conceptions of history characteristically raises more questions than it answers, it does not simply leave us lost among the thorns and dangers of a meaningless world with no suggestions for finding our way. The questions I attend to here have most to do with the past's effective value for the present that remembers it, and most particularly with the viability of memories that are inspired to revive former greatness in present action and thus renew lost leaders for the benefit of the living. As we shall see (and as I have already suggested), these questions become more intrinsically involved with the validity of such memories—with their falsifications and their fictions—as we move from the first tetralogy through *King John* and the second tetralogy.[12] As the questions become more complex, so do the responses they evoke. Again, I would insist that the final play in this series cannot be taken as Shakespeare's last word on its subjects. I will argue, however, that when Henry V, who began the first of the histories as the lamented lost leader, finally emerges in his own play as the series' last embodiment of the hero, both living and "valiant dead," he is presented in terms that take into account the preceding plays' questions about the uses of the past and that offer us, with respect to them, a viable way to "remember with advantages."

These Valiant Dead

1 Henry VI

"From Their Ashes Shall Be Reared / A Phoenix"

The first play of the first tetralogy begins with the most plaintive and extended lament for a lost leader that we will encounter through the entire series of English history plays. Bedford's opening lines intensify the solemnity of Henry V's funeral procession by sounding the enormity of both the loss and its consequences:

> Hung be the heavens with black, yield day to night!
> Comets, importing change of times and states,
> Brandish your crystal tresses in the sky
> And with them scourge the bad revolting stars
> That have consented unto Henry's death—

King Henry the Fifth, too famous to live long!
England ne'er lost a king of so much worth.

For fifty-six lines, ruffled only by a brief but ominous flurry between Winchester and Gloucester, the bereaved lords dwell on the
virtues of the deceased ("his deeds exceed all speech"), the grim
finality of his passing ("Henry is dead and never shall revive"),
and England's abject helplessness without him ("arms avail not,
now that Henry's dead").

The bleak negatives that cloud the prospect of an England
without Henry are, for all their funeral-baked hyperboles, perfectly valid.[1] There *will* be a "change of times and states" undoing
all that Henry had so gloriously accomplished. And, in dramatic
rather than historical terms, this play will dwindle to a pathetically
ironic and inconclusive ending (suited to the emasculated England Bedford foresees in lines 48–51) that subverts the heroic
tragedy of Talbot's death, just as Bedford's soaring eulogy to
Henry V's ghost is abruptly undercut in this opening scene by
messengers coming in with the first waves of the bad news that
will flood the entire tetralogy. "Lost" is the appropriate keynote
for the leaderless world that Henry's death leaves to its factious
devices here.

But the devastation of England without its hero king is tem-
pered, particularly in this first play, by the positive potential for
sustaining and reviving his grand heritage that is kept in view.
Even in the sequels, as the nation's self-inflicted wounds fester
under the malignant shadow of Richard Gloucester, the dramatized rupture between the grim present and its better past is never
so radically unsettling as it will prove to be in *Richard II*. And
Part One illustrates more positively than any other play until
Henry V's own (and more simply than that later play) how the
leader of the past can survive as a vital presence in those who
properly emulate (and thus renew) him in the present. Such a
possibility directly counters and complicates what would other-

wise stand simply as the most tautological platitude uttered at Henry's funeral: "Henry is dead and never shall revive" (18).[2]

The idea that England's heroic historical heritage can live anew in the present is first voiced early in the play by the awed enemy. The French, having just boasted fatuously of their newfound ascendancy over the "famished English," are comically reduced by the ensuing rout and, as Alençon's haughty ridicule converts to wondering admiration, he evokes for the first time the storied epoch of Edward III that will serve so often through both tetralogies as an emblem of England's past glory:

> Froissart, a countryman of ours, records
> England all Olivers and Rowlands bred
> During the time Edward the Third did reign.
> More truly now may this be verified,
> For none but Samsons and Goliases
> It sendeth forth to skirmish.
>
> (I, ii, 29–34)

This identification of past and present English prowess in such mythical terms is, as I will argue later, noteworthy in itself. But it is not for a facile Frenchman to uphold alone the tradition of English valor at its proper worth. That, of course, is first and foremost the role of Talbot, who keeps the heroic spirit of Henry V alive in this play. Were others to share that enterprise with him, as the entire play makes clear, the great leader would not be "lost" at all but would "revive" indeed. Fittingly, the opening scene divides its focus between the dead and living heroes, turning from the lament for Henry to news of Talbot's (for once unfortunate) exploits in France. As a loyal soldier and servant of the crown, Talbot cannot of course replace the king himself, but he can and does maintain the heroic heritage of that king, and his current deeds ("where valiant Talbot above human thought / Enacted wonders with his sword and lance") are accorded from the beginning something akin to the superhuman stature Henry's mourners recall in the victor of Agincourt:

> His brandished sword did blind men with his beams;
> His arms spread wider than a dragon's wings;
> His sparkling eyes, replete with wrathful fire,
> More dazzled and drove back his enemies
> Than midday sun fierce bent against their faces.
>
> (I, i, 121–122, 10–14)

In his first actual appearance, Talbot virtually enacts the process of renewing in his own person the valiant dead who precede him. While he is surveying the besieged Orléans from a turret with the earl of Salisbury, the latter is shot, and Talbot effectively assumes the spirit of the dying hero as he eulogizes him:

> Speak, Salisbury; at least if thou canst speak.
> How far'st thou, mirror of all martial men?
>
> .   .   .   .
>
> In thirteen battles Salisbury o'ercame;
> Henry the Fifth he first trained to the wars.
> Whilst any trump did sound or drum struck up
> His sword did ne'er leave striking in the field.
> Yet liv'st thou, Salisbury?
>
> .   .   .   .   .   .
>
> He beckons with his hand and smiles on me,
> As who should say, "When I am dead and gone,
> Remember to avenge me on the French."
> Plantagenet, I will, and like thee,
> Play on the lute, beholding the towns burn.
> Wretched shall France be only in my name.
>
> .   .   .   .
>
> Frenchmen, I'll be a Salisbury to you.
>
> (I, iv, 73–106)

The exemplary "mirror of all martial men" who first tutored Henry V himself in the art of war will continue, now that he and

Henry are both dead, to inspire others as he is reflected in Talbot. Retaining his own potent heroic identity ("Wretched shall France be only in my name"), Talbot will also keep Salisbury's alive by emulating him ("Frenchmen, I'll be a Salisbury to you"). Thus, Salisbury's affectionate greeting as they first entered—"Talbot, my life, my joy, again returned?"—will prove true in this extended sense. In the ensuing scenes, after a temporary setback at the be-witched hands of Joan de Pucelle, Talbot carries out his vow to the letter. His "name only" *does* send the French scurrying (II, i, 77), and as he enters the reconquered Orléans, he ensures that Salisbury will continue to live (along with Talbot himself) as a "mirror of all martial men" for future ages:

> Bring forth the body of old Salisbury
> And here advance it in the market place,
> The middle center of this cursèd town.
> Now have I paid my vow unto his soul:
> For every drop of blood was drawn from him
> There hath at least five Frenchmen died to-night.
> And that hereafter ages may behold
> What ruin happened in revenge of him,
> Within their chiefest temple I'll erect
> A tomb, wherein his corpse shall be interred;
> Upon the which, that every one may read,
> Shall be engraved the sack of Orleans,
> The treacherous manner of his mournful death,
> And what a terror he had been to France.
>
>   (II, ii, 4–17)

Through such means history's valiant dead are not lost, but live in memory for the present and for "hereafter ages."

I may seem to juggle terms and blur distinctions here, since "old Salisbury" is not strictly a "historical" figure for Talbot in the same sense that Edward III was or that both Salisbury and Talbot himself are for Shakespeare's audience. He is, rather, an older col-league whom Talbot succeeds, much as one generation succeeds another. For Talbot, however, and for the use of the historic past that he illustrates here, that is a distinction without a difference. Salisbury, like Talbot himself, serves as an inspirational mirror in life and, remembered as Talbot remembers him ("Now, Salisbury, for thee . . ." [II, i, 35]), continues as such to his immediate successors and "hereafter ages" alike. Thus Talbot, assaulting Rouen, calls on the recently dead Henry V and the long dead Richard I as equally living presences along with the young king he now serves:

> And I, as sure as English Henry lives
> And as his father here was conqueror,
> As sure as in this late betrayèd town
> Great Coeur-de-lion's heart was burièd,
> So sure I swear to get the town or die.
>   (III, ii, 80–84)

And the ailing Bedford, in the same scene, looks farther back in British lore for a precedent that will sustain his gallant refusal to leave the field, just as his living example will "revive" the hearts of the soldiers who have ever taken him as their "mirror":

> *Burgundy*: Courageous Bedford, let us now persuade you.
> *Bedford*: Not to be gone from hence; for once I read
> That stout Pendragon in his litter sick
> Came to the field and vanquishèd his foes.
> Methinks I should revive the soldiers' hearts,
> Because I ever found them as myself.
>   (93–98)

The gallant old man dies but his spirit remains "undaunted" (99), and Talbot characteristically insists that he be remembered:

> But yet, before we go, let's not forget
> The noble Duke of Bedford, late deceased,
> But see his exequies fulfilled in Roan.

A braver soldier never couchèd lance,
A gentler heart did never sway in court.
                    (131–135)

"Let's not forget." That is the impulse through which the heroic
past lives on in the present. And though both Bedford and Talbot
sound muted *de casibus* notes here ("What is the trust or strength
of foolish man?"; "But kings and mightiest potentates must die, /
For that's the end of human misery" [112, 136–137]), and thereby
slightly modify the primary strain of "noble deeds as valor's monuments" (120), it is the latter that rings out here for us above all.

In the scenes given to Talbot's heroic death, in fact, renewal
through generational succession and through the longer reach of
historic fame *are* brought into conflict, and the latter supersedes
the former at the insistence of young John Talbot, whose gallant
refusal to abandon his father we are asked to applaud. Looking
toward his own regeneration in the future exploits of his son,
Talbot realizes that the boy's intended initiation to arms outside
the walls of Bordeaux will in fact be a hopeless catastrophe:

O young John Talbot, I did send for thee
To tutor thee in stratagems of war,
That Talbot's name *might be in thee revived*
When sapless age and weak unable limbs
Should bring thy father to his drooping chair.
But O malignant and ill-boding stars!
Now thou art come unto a feast of death,
A terrible and unavoided danger.
Therefore, dear boy, mount on my swiftest horse,
And I'll direct thee how thou shalt escape
By sudden flight. Come, dally not, be gone.
                    (IV, v, 1–11; emphasis added)

But the boy, against all the urgings of his father in a debate that
stretches through two scenes, opts for "mortality / Rather than

life preserved with infamy" (IV, v, 32–33). In the brief time of the battle itself, young John's heroics do reinvigorate his father:

> When from the Dauphin's crest thy sword struck fire,
> It warmed thy father's heart with proud desire
> Of bold-faced victory. Then leaden age,
> Quickened with youthful spleen and warlike rage,
> Beat down Alençon, Orleans, Burgundy,
> And from the pride of Gallia rescued thee.
>
> (IV, vi, 10–15)

But in the longer reach of history, by dying so gloriously, young John surmounts death and gains, with his father, the immortality of "bright fame":

> Thou antic Death, which laugh'st us here to scorn,
> Anon, from thy insulting tyranny,
> Coupled in bonds of perpetuity,
> Two Talbots, wingèd through the lither sky,
> In thy despite shall scape mortality.
>
> (IV, vii, 18–22)

With the counterpoint that is already his hallmark, Shakespeare allows Joan a nasty deflation of the grand list of names Lucy then rehearses over the fallen hero and his son:

> Here's a silly stately style indeed!
>
> .   .   .   .
>
> Him that thou magnifi'st with all these titles,
> Stinking and flyblown lies here at our feet.
>
> (IV, vii, 72–76)

Lucy, however, has the last (and, for our topic, most significant) word on the subject: "I'll bear them hence; but from their ashes shall be reared / A phoenix that shall make all France afeard" (92–93). More important than the fact that this prophecy is not fulfilled in this play or its sequels (though, in violation of historical chronology, *Henry V* provides its ultimate dramatic fulfillment), or that it may still be left open-ended for the Elizabethan audience, is the play's confident affirmation of this potential for renewal. Whoever he may be and whenever he appears, the "future" English hero will be the reincarnation of these fifteenth-century heirs to "the time Edward the Third did reign" and so on back to "stout Pendragon." Whatever "change of times and states" may transpire, the play, like Talbot himself, affirms this fundamental continuity between past and present which can be realized in the person of any hero who revives the spirit of his predecessors and thereby identifies himself with them.[3]

If Talbot is by all odds the play's most positive force, he is, however, by no means the dominant force in the play. He may triumph over death, but his death is caused by those Englishmen who are opposed to him in every essential respect and who, as the Salisburys and Bedfords and Talbots die out, gain ever more perilous ascendancy. From the first scene on, this play is built simply and solidly on the absolute contrast between Talbot and the host of wrangling lords who bring on England's woes (the Woes of the Roses). It would distort the play in behalf of my subject to argue that the very heart of this contrast lay in the opposed parties' respective attitudes toward the past. More fundamental to it, as any audience must realize, is the factionalism based on willful self-interest that is the very opposite of Talbot's single-minded service to his king and his country. It takes no greater personage than the first messenger in the first scene to point directly at the root of all this play's evil in an English court that should know and do better:

> Amongst the soldiers this is mutterèd,
> That here you maintain several factions,
> And whilst a field should be dispatched and fought
> You are disputing of your generals.
>
> (70–73)

And Exeter, evidently having nothing else to do in the play, steps forth periodically as chorus to drive home the already obvious point about such "factious bandying" (IV, i, 190) and the ashes in which it smolders, so very different from those that will spawn Talbot's phoenix:

> This late dissension grown betwixt the peers
> Burns under feignèd ashes of forged love
> And will at last break out into a flame.
> As fest'red members rot but by degree
> Till bones and flesh and sinews fall away,
> So will this base and envious discord breed.
>   (III, i, 188–193)

The fundamental cause of this dissension is the primacy of self-centered "will" above all else, not a misguided attitude toward (or use of) the past, and all those who are guided by this basic motive see (as Richard Plantagenet does) "growing time" ripening according to *their* will (II, iv, 99), whereas we see plainly, with Exeter, that the times are festering (rather than ripening) from the disease of dissension.

Nonetheless, in the stark opposition between Talbot's better way and the factionalists' worse, as we move back and forth between his exploits in France and their turmoil in England, the radically different uses of memory and history are a prominent and symptomatic feature of the contrast. When the two major parties-to-be first square off in the Temple Garden and choose those "dumb significants" of their antagonism, the essentially meaningless white and red roses, the priority of will over any legal basis in historical fact is openly asserted by the lords on both sides, who show an arrogant and aristocratic disdain for such ink-horn scholarship:

> *Suffolk*: Faith, I have been a truant in the law
> And never yet could frame my will to it,

And therefore frame the law unto my will.
Somerset: Judge you, my Lord of Warwick, then
   between us.
Warwick: Between two hawks, which flies the higher pitch,
Between two dogs, which hath the deeper mouth,
Between two blades, which bears the better temper,
Between two horses, which doth bear him best,
Between two girls, which hath the merriest eye,
I have perhaps some shallow spirit of judgment;
But in these nice sharp quillets of the law,
Good faith, I am no wiser than a daw.

(II, iv, 7–18)

But once they have already lined up against one another on the basis of conflicting and unspecified "truths" that each side claims to be self-evident (20–24), these same lords use historical "facts" readily enough as weapons to hurl at one another rather than as a means to resolve the rights or wrongs of the case:

Warwick: Now, by God's will, thou wrong'st him,
   Somerset.
His grandfather was Lionel Duke of Clarence,
Third son to the third Edward, King of England.
Spring crestless yeoman from so deep a root?
Richard: He bears him on the place's privilege,
Or durst not for his craven heart say thus.
Somerset: By him that made me, I'll maintain my words
On any plot of ground in Christendom.
Was not thy father, Richard Earl of Cambridge,
For treason executed in our late king's days?
And by his treason stand'st not thou attainted,
Corrupted, and exempt from ancient gentry?
His trespass yet lives guilty in thy blood,
And till thou be restored thou art a yeoman.
Richard: My father was attachèd, not attainted,

Condemned to die for treason, but no traitor;
And that I'll prove on better men than Somerset,
Were growing time once ripened to my will.
For your partaker Pole, and you yourself,
I'll note you in my book of memory
To scourge you for this apprehension.
Look to it well and say you are well warned.

(82–103)

The threatening context in which he uses the term here suggests what function Richard's "book of memory" serves first and foremost.

Note that the "third Edward, King of England" becomes, in such a dispute, no more than the deep root of a genealogical tree rather than the famous ruler of that time when "England all Olivers and Rowlands bred," as he is remembered in France, where Talbot wages the good fight, or of that time "when first this order [of the Garter] was ordained" and "knights of the Garter were of noble birth, / Valiant and virtuous, full of haughty courage," as Talbot himself will recall it (IV, i, 33–35). The issue here, as the play emphasizes it, is not so much which faction may be right in its historical arguments, and certainly not that genealogy and legal history are pernicious studies in and of themselves. The clear point, rather (and it scarcely simplifies this play, as it would most of Shakespeare's, to speak of its "point" in this regard), is that the factionalists use their history and their memories willfully, destructively, and hence wrongly, whereas Talbot uses his historical precedents positively as models for heroic action.

As is this play's way, the point is amplified through successive scenes. Richard visits his dying uncle Mortimer to complain, in a pun that is glaringly obvious to everyone in the theater except himself, of his "dis-ease" (II, v, 44). Mortimer is a ruined relic of the past that Richard probes here, and the young aspirant's faith that "growing time" will ripen to his will might be daunted by the gloomy spectacle of his uncle's "decaying age" (1). Instead, of course, he eagerly seizes the heritage Mortimer proffers him as a prop and stimulant for his ever-dominant will:

> And therefore haste I to the parliament,
> Either to be restorèd to my blood
> Or make my will th'advantage of my good.
>
> (127–129)

Mortimer is the first actual "historian" in the histories, and his anti-Lancastrian review of the succession from Edward III through Henry VI, correct enough in its essential facts despite its clear bias (and Shakespeare's relatively inconsequential confusion of Mortimers), is allowed to stand uncontested by any Lancastrian counterpart or rebuttal in the play. But that does not mean we line up here with Richard, even though he shares his private thoughts with us more consistently than does any other character. Those private thoughts, like Winchester's at the end of the first scene, expose Richard's selfish and dangerous ambition to us rather than engage us in his point of view.[4] The play is simply less interested in the constitutional issues of the Yorkist-Lancastrian conflict than it is in the motives, attitudes, and actions of the contestants on either side. To be on a "side" first and foremost, and thereby to foment factional strife, is the great wrong here, by contrast with Talbot's simple loyalty to king, country, and the heroic heritage he upholds. The significant contrast between Talbot's remembrance of the past and Mortimer's (or Richard's via Mortimer) is the use each makes of his greater and lesser forebears. Edward III and Henry V, whose times and deeds shine with heroic precedents for Talbot, shrink in Mortimer's account to the same stature as their disappointing successors, Richard II and Henry VI. Their accomplishments mean nothing. They "count" only insofar as their standing on the genealogical chart proves the speaker's claim to the throne.

The foreseeable consequences of rampant self-interest that may use history for its own purposes (but is scarcely inspired by it) are "so plain" that the choral Exeter wishes himself dead before they can come to pass (III, i, 199–200). The immediate result is the downfall of Talbot, and, with no survivors to remember and replace him as he "renewed" Salisbury, the ruin of the realm follows. As Talbot falls, so does the remembrance of the valiant dead that he embodied. Lucy, frustrated by those "great commanders" York and Somerset, whose mutual antagonism betrays Talbot "to loss," sums up the whole sorry story and its larger implications:

> Thus, while the vulture of sedition
> Feeds in the bosom of such great commanders,
> Sleeping neglection doth betray to loss
> The conquest of our scarce-cold conqueror,
> That ever-living man of memory,
> Henry the Fifth. Whiles they each other cross,
> Lives, honors, lands, and all hurry to loss.
>
> (IV, iii, 47–53)

The play's priorities—its sense of the truly crucial rights and wrongs—are perfectly clear here as elsewhere. Whatever the constitutional legitimacy of the Lancastrian rulership, Henry V's heroic heritage is above all to be remembered, preserved, and renewed, not neglected "to loss." Only thus can the historical hero be "that ever-living man of memory," or be so to any good purpose. Likewise, in his own degree, with Talbot. But "sleeping neglection" not only causes his downfall; it quashes out any recollection of him thereafter. The play, of course, memorializes and thus renews him in his own spirit, as Nashe testifies:

> How would it have joyed brave *Talbot* (the terror of the French) to thinke that after he had lyne two hundred yeares in his Tombe, hee should triumphe againe on the Stage, and have his bones newe embalmed with the teares

of ten thousand spectators at least (at severall times), who,
in the Tragedian that represents his person, imagine they
behold him fresh bleeding.[5]

In this way, in representational art if not in historical deed,
Shakespeare's "tragedian" becomes the phoenix Lucy foresaw. But
in the play, after Lucy's eulogy, Talbot is totally forgotten. Though
we should be reminded of him by such dramatic devices as the
sharp contrast between Joan's death and his (she denies her father
and dies wretchedly; he embraces his son and dies heroically), no
one onstage remembers him or utters his name. In such "sleeping
neglection" of the heritage that might redeem its England, the
play "ends" (rather than concludes) with a pointed anticipation of
even worse troubles to come.[6]

This dismal prospect, however, still remains unclouded by factors that will complicate the represented "change of times and
states" in later histories. If all the play's plain signs (buttressed by
our historical foreknowledge) validate the various prophecies of
disaster beyond any shadow of doubt, there is nothing in the
nature of things as we see it here suggesting that it had to be
so, that it could not have been otherwise. Nothing more substantial, that is, than Joan's theory, summoned in support of her own
cause, that "glory is like a circle in the water, / Which never ceaseth
to enlarge itself / Till by broad spreading it disperse to naught. /
With Henry's death the English circle ends" (I, ii, 133–136).
From the opening scene on, everything in the presentation indicates that the contentious lords who burst the circle of England's
glory both can and should know and do otherwise, and that no fundamental evolution from a better heroic past to a lesser pedestrian
present need take place. Both Talbot and his erring opposites are
presented in exemplary colors that imply the full potential in them
(as in the audience that watches and should learn from them) for
realizing the better way and its happier consequences. In this way,
1 Henry VI not only shows us (in Talbot) the proper way of using

history but *is* inspirational history, awakening remembrance of the valiant dead with the clear-eyed confidence of Talbot himself.[7]

Nor is the presentation of this inspirational model colored with any suggestion of fictionalization or idealization that would either distance the hero from the actual world of the audience or question the authenticity of his historical image as we see it here. Lucy's speech looks out from the play to the world of the audience with the full implication that the "phoenix" who will revive Talbot may (and can) appear there, suggesting perfect continuity between the dramatized past and the spectators' present. And however good Talbot is, there is no hint in the play that he is too good to be true. Quite the opposite. The countess of Auvergne does think, on first view, that the "real" Talbot she sees scarcely matches the storied hero of whom she has heard:

> Is this the scourge of France?
> Is this the Talbot, so much feared abroad
> That with his name the mothers still their babes?
> I see report is fabulous and false.
> I thought I should have seen some Hercules,
> A second Hector, for his grim aspect
> And large proportion of his strong-knit limbs.
> Alas, this is a child, a silly dwarf.
> It cannot be this weak and writhled shrimp
> Should strike such terror to his enemies.
>   (II, iii, 16–24)

But, as she realizes when Talbot adroitly supplements his "shadow" with the "substance" of his soldiers and thereby foils her hope to become a second Tomyris by trapping him, the countess is sorely mistaken:

> Victorious Talbot, pardon my abuse.
> I find thou art no less than fame hath bruited,
> And more than may be gathered by thy shape.
>   (67–69)

If any disparity exists between the Talbot we see onstage and the "real" Talbot, the last line here suggests that it must be in the latter's favor. But such questions are scarcely essential. This first in Shakespeare's series of histories renews Talbot's fame with every implication that its hero, if "lost" to those factionalists who neglected him and his better way to their country's detriment, now lives anew both in the play and (potentially) in any auditor who will properly emulate him.[8]

CHAPTER TWO

2 & 3 Henry VI

"Undoing All as All Had Never Been"

The lament opening *1 Henry VI* was for the lost leader and the foreseen "change of times and states" in an England bereft of him. But there had been no thought then that all that Henry had been and done might itself vanish. Rather, he would shine as "a far more glorious star . . . / Than Julius Caesar" (55–56). As we have seen, however, Lucy later deplores the "sleeping neglection" that threatens to cancel out the conquests of this "ever-living man of memory" (IV, iii, 49–51). And as Part Two opens with a nuptial scene that is at least as ominous as the funeral with which Part One began, Gloucester warns his fellow (but scarcely collegial) peers that the past itself and not just its hero king is in danger of dying:

What? Did my brother Henry spend his youth,
His valor, coin, and people in the wars?
Did he so often lodge in open field,
In winter's cold and summer's parching heat,
To conquer France, his true inheritance?

. . . .

And shall these labors and these honors die?
Shall Henry's conquest, Bedford's vigilance,
Your deeds of war, and all our counsel die?
O peers of England, shameful is this league.
Fatal this marriage, cancelling your fame,
Blotting your names from books of memory.
Rasing the characters of your renown,
Defacing monuments of conquered France,
Undoing all as all had never been!

(76–101)

The eradicating process Gloucester envisions as the result of Henry's foolish marriage to the dowerless Margaret is, of course, the exact inverse of Talbot's efforts at heroic renewal. Against such blotting, rasing, and defacing, Talbot's erection of a monument to Salisbury in the marketplace of Orléans, where he had revived Salisbury's spirit through his own conquest, stands as a positive (and literal) model.

Gloucester's "passionate discourse" is, given his honest but splenetic temper, characteristically hyperbolic. The very existence of the play in which he voices them proves that his fears of being blotted, along with the other sharers in Henry V's glory, "from books of memory" will not ultimately be realized. And we will see more clearly the limited significance given here to such "undoing" of the past when we explore the dramatization of that process in *Richard II*. Nonetheless, Gloucester's outburst offers an appropriate keynote for the second and third parts of *Henry VI*, where not only are recent English accomplishments undone but virtually no positive memory of the English past survives. These are history plays about a nation that has little sense (and makes no good use) of its own history.

Like Gloucester, I am indulging in hyperbole for the sake of emphasis here. It should be recalled, in behalf of responsible accuracy, that York enlists the support of the Nevils (Warwick and Salisbury) by rehearsing his historical claim in such intricate detail that few modern audiences are likely to exclaim, with Warwick, "What plain proceedings is more plain than this?" (II, ii, 10–58). I can reiterate the point already made about the Yorkist recourse to genealogy in Part One—that it reduces heroes and goats alike to flat factors in the reckoning ("Edward the Black Prince died before his father / And left behind him Richard, his only son"). The difference is that this is the *only* sort of recollection of England's famous fourteenth-century victors in this play and its sequel. Neither the Black Prince nor his "mountain sire" (nor such an earlier figure as Richard Cordelion) is evoked to celebrate his heritage or inspire emulation. With minimal exceptions (to be noted shortly) in the case of Henry V, no such use of England's past glory is made whatsoever through these two long plays.

Moreover, even more pointedly than in Part One, the recourse to legal history itself proves superficial rather than fundamental, a matter of political tactics that shows no true regard for the constitutional past. York makes less and less of it, even as a selling point, as he pursues his claim, relying more both privately and publicly on the Tamburlainian ground of his merit and Henry's weakness:

> Nor shall proud Lancaster usurp my right,
> Nor hold the sceptre in his childish fist,
> Nor wear the diadem upon his head,
> Whose churchlike humors fits not for a crown.
>
> (2, I, i, 242–245)

> No! thou art not king,
> Not fit to govern and rule multitudes,

Which dar'st not, no, nor canst not rule a traitor.

That head of thine doth not become a crown;

Thy hand is made to grasp a palmer's staff

And not to grace an awful princely sceptre.

That gold must round engirt these brows
of mine,

Whose smile and frown, like to Achilles' spear,

Is able with the change to kill and cure.

Here is a hand to hold a sceptre up

And with the same to act controlling laws.

Give place. By heaven, thou shalt rule no more

O'er him whom heaven created for thy ruler.

(2, V, i, 93–105)

It had been clear, of course, from York's first utterance of his aspirations in Part One that personal will surmounted whatever historical "right" might be used to support it. And his priorities in this regard are shared by all alike in Parts Two and Three. Young Clifford's disregard for constitutional issues is exceptional only for its outright candor: "King Henry, be thy title right or wrong, / Lord Clifford vows to fight in thy defense" (3, I, i, 159–160). Oxford, who offers the only substantial historical justification of the Lancastrian claim in the entire trilogy (3, III, iii, 81–87), steps out from behind it when pressed and reveals the true basis of his partisanship:

Call him [Edward] my king by whose injurious doom

My elder brother, the Lord Aubrey Vere,

Was done to death? and more than so, my father,

Even in the downfall of his mellowed years,

When nature brought him to the door of death?

No, Warwick, no! While life upholds this arm,

This arm upholds the house of Lancaster.

(101–107)

And Warwick, whose allegiance to York may appear more a matter of constitutional principle than is that of any other major figure on either side (see 2, II, ii, 53–62), subordinates that principle to his personal honor (or pride) as soon as he feels the latter to be injured by his presumably rightful monarch:

> Had he [Edward] none else to make a stale but me?
> Then none but I shall turn his jest to sorrow.
> I was the chief that raised him to the crown
> And I'll be chief to bring him down again;
> Not that I pity Henry's misery,
> But seek revenge on Edward's mockery.
>
> (3, III, iii, 260–265)

His last line here expresses what has become the dominant motive on both sides—revenge. To the extent that historical right to the throne is debated at all in the "Bloody Parliament" scene which opens Part Three, the nod surely is given to York, both by Henry's concession ("I know not what to say; my title's weak" [134]) and by the apparently just-minded Exeter's defection ("His [York's] is the right, and therefore pardon me" [148]). But Exeter, an anomaly of impartiality in this sharply divided world, points out why neither constitutionality nor any gesture of compromise can possibly sway the hard-core Lancastrians: "They seek revenge and therefore will not yield" (190).

Revenge, of course, implies the implacable memory that fuels it, and to a large extent it would be fair to say that revenge replaces heroic renewal here as the primary use of the past to "inspire" present action. As early as the second act of Part One, Richard Plantagenet had given notice of the prominence that this intensely personalized "book of memory" (as distinct from the public and celebrative "books of memory" Gloucester sees being erased) assumes in the world he helps to shake apart:

> For your partaker Pole, and you [Somerset] yourself,
> I'll note you in my book of memory

To scourge you for this apprehension.
Look to it well and say you are well warned.

(II, iv, 100–103)

And "Bloody Clifford" becomes the embodiment of this common motive, dedicating himself over his fallen father to the single-minded cause of vengeance:

> Even at this sight
> My heart is turned to stone; and while 'tis mine,
> It shall be stony. York not our old men spares;
> No more will I their babes. Tears virginal
> Shall be to me even as the dew to fire;
> And beauty, that the tyrant oft reclaims,
> Shall to my flaming wrath be oil and flax.
> Henceforth I will not have to do with pity.
> Meet I an infant of the house of York,
> Into as many gobbets will I cut it
> As wild Medea young Absyrtus did.
> In cruelty will I seek out my fame.

(2, V, ii, 49–60)

As "good" as his word, he slaughters the pathetic young Rutland in pursuit of the only cause he cares for:

> *Clifford*: Thy father slew my father. Therefore die.
> *Rutland*: Di faciant laudis summa sit ista tuae!

(3, I, iii, 47–48)

Both as he makes his vow and as he fulfills it, Clifford stands as an antitype—or at the very best as a savage degeneration—of the ideal Talbot had upheld in his remembrance of the fallen Salisbury. Heroic renewal is degraded into destructive vengeance, and Rutland's Ovidian prayer, echoing Clifford's own relegation of his "fame" to such heartless "cruelty," may call to mind the different intention realized in Talbot's monument to Salisbury.[1] Likewise, the prophecy York hurls at his captors, even as it echoes Lucy's prophecy over the dead Talbots, emphasizes the turn from heroic renewal to personal revenge: "My ashes, as the phoenix, may bring forth / A bird that will revenge upon you all" (3, I, iv, 35–36).

But to say that revenge replaces renewal as memory's motive (or as the focus of memory) is still to miss an important part of the distinction between Talbot's heroic ideal and the presented behavior of those who succeed and forget him. Despite revenge's ubiquity in Parts Two and Three, remembrance plays a relatively minor role in its execution. True, Clifford's memory of his father's blood stops the passage where Rutland's pleading words should enter (3, I, iii, 21–22). But here, and even more exclusively in most instances, the revenger's focus is forward, on the object of his hatred, not backward, memorializing its cause. As York and his ashy phoenix imply, revenge's cycle does foster a destructive kind of continuity (York kills Clifford; Clifford's son kills York and York's son; York's other sons kill young Clifford). But its thrust, as we see it here, is ever onward. When the ominous bird of York's prophecy takes its final flight in *Richard III*, the primary pattern of retribution will be highlighted through recollections of the dreadful past—the awful history that takes its inexorable toll on that play's present. In these two plays, however, where that "history" is itself taking place, vengeance scarcely keeps the past alive even in the minds of those who pursue it. Here, rather than serving as a vehicle to carry the remembered past into the present, personal revenge tends to stifle whatever recourse to history might otherwise make its claim on these contentious lords' allegiance. Warwick's reversal at the French court is symptomatic in this respect.

Though the memory of such a recent hero as Talbot and all recollections of earlier English valor are blotted, rased, and defaced from the vengeful and ambitious minds that dominate here, Henry V's heritage cannot be totally ignored by those who squabble over his leavings. Still, it is surprising how little positive use even the Lan-

castrians make of "that ever-living man of memory." True, Henry
is repeatedly recalled by way of blaming his singularly unambi-
tious and charitable son for not being like him. But the focus here
is always reproach for what has been lost, never encouragement to
emulation, as we see when the dying Clifford switches the blame
from father to son in the application of his sunny simile:

> O Phoebus, hadst thou never given consent
> That Phaeton should check thy fiery steeds,
> Thy burning car never had scorched the earth!
> And, Henry, hadst thou swayed as kings should do,
> Or as thy father and his father did,
> Giving no ground unto the house of York,
> They never then had sprung like summer flies.
>
> $\qquad\qquad\qquad\qquad$ (3, II, vi, 11–17)

Even when Clifford does exhort his reluctant leader to be made
of sterner stuff and cites Henry IV and Henry V in the process,
he cites them only as the winners of all that Henry VI is giving
away, not as role models. Rather, in keeping with his own fero-
cious spirit, Clifford holds up the lion, the forest bear, the lurking
serpent, and all such "unreasonable creatures" for poor Henry to
imitate in defense of his son's birthright: "Make them your precedent" (3, II, ii, 9–42). Henry is provoked into responding with
the tetralogy's most radical statement on the whole question of
heritage: "I'll leave my son my virtuous deeds behind, / And
would my father had left me no more" (49–50). But the potentially positive alternative to inherited martial heroics that glim-
mers briefly in these lines is subverted, as in Henry's other saintly
moments, by clear indications that he is shrinking (half-petulantly
here) from his proper responsibility:

> For all the rest is held at such a rate
> As brings a thousandfold more care to keep
> Than in possession any jot of pleasure.
>
> $\qquad\qquad\qquad\qquad$ (51–53)

Only twice in the long course of these two plays is Henry V recalled in something like the terms of renewal and inspiration that informed Talbot's heroic ideal, and in both instances irony crowds in from the prevailing context. Toward the end of Part Three, Oxford sees the lineaments of the hero king reborn in his grandson, the Lancastrian Prince Edward:

> O brave young prince, thy famous grandfather
> Doth live again in thee. Long mayst thou live
> To bear his image and renew his glories.
>
> (V, iv, 52–54)

But Oxford's bright hope only sets up the cruel reversal of the very next scene in which Edward of York, finding the captured young prince's likeness in his railing mother rather than his famous grandfather, leads his eager brothers' murderous assault on the boy. And toward the end of Part Two, Clifford Senior had used the name of "Henry Fifth that made all France to quake" to rally Cade's mob back into obedience to the hero's hapless heir. It takes no keener observer than Cade himself, however, to estimate accurately the inspirational force at work here: "Was ever feather so lightly blown to and fro as this multitude?" (IV, viii, 15–54).

Even Cade shows some deference to "Henry the Fifth (in whose time boys went to span-counter for French crowns)" (IV, ii, 145–146). But far from showing what would be, in these plays, a rare susceptibility to the call of heroic history, the mob in general and Cade in particular parody the disregard for history's authority that pervades the nobility, just as they parody other failings in their "betters." Their larger hostility to learning of any kind, which prompts them to execute everyone who can read and write, caricatures the aristocratic disdain for "nice sharp quillets of the law" that surfaced in Part One's seminal Temple Garden scene. And they threaten to carry out literally the "undoing" of all "books of memory" that Gloucester had so dreaded: "Away, burn all the records of the realm! My mouth shall be the parliament of

England" (IV, vii, 11–13). Cade's proclamation is only a blunt extension of York's assertion of will over law or Clifford's avowed disregard for the "right or wrong" of the Lancastrian title he supports. Though Cade does not quite achieve his ultimate solution, he and his "men of Kent" manage to "undo" history in their execution of the learned Lord Say, who appeals to them through the hopeful authority of recorded history:

> Hear me but speak, and bear me where'er you will.
> Kent, in the Commentaries Caesar writ,
> Is termed the civil'st place of all this isle.
> Sweet is the country, because full of riches;
> The people liberal, valiant, active, wealthy,
> Which makes me hope you are not void of pity.
>
> (IV, vii, 53–58)

Cade blots out such hope and effectually contradicts the history on which it is based by beheading Lord Say "an it be but for pleading so well for his life" (98–99).

Given the current state of the government against which they rebel, the mob's grievances are not without their telling points. But whatever truth leaks through their complaint that "the king's council are no good workmen" (IV, ii, 12–13) scarcely sustains their "larger" vision of England's past, present, and future. Concerns that will be given serious consideration in later history plays are reduced here to comic absurdity as Cade and his followers voice them. One such concern is the nostalgic sense of a better past, of a world transformed from what it once was and still ought to be, that will figure so prominently in *Richard II*. The mob's appeal to "ancient freedom," to a "merry world" before "gentlemen came up" (IV, viii, 25; ii, 7–8), has nothing of history or memory about it, of course. It flows, rather, with the same impulse that would obliterate all actual history and any record thereof in quest of an Edenic Utopia wherein "all the realm shall be in common" (IV, ii, 62). But if this impulse to cancel "all as all had never been" reflects grotesquely the "sleeping neglection" that blots all recollection of England's heroic heritage among the factious nobles, the mob's sense of a world (or an England) transformed for the worse finds no echo in any higher consciousness in these two plays. Everyone can see that Henry VI falls woefully short of his father, and we watch a process of obvious deterioration as even the familial ties that bound "bloody Clifford" to his father break down and Richard of Gloucester slouches closer to the controlling center of the stage. But, in the general paucity of retrospect, no one seriously recalls a better English past now lost. The only loss widely lamented is that of the lands Henry V had won in France.[2]

The other major concern of the second tetralogy that is comically adumbrated through Cade here is the fictive reconstruction of history. When William Stafford accuses Cade of learning from the duke of York the genealogy by which he dubs himself Lord Mortimer, Cade sardonically remarks aside, "He lies, for I invented it myself" (IV, ii, 142–143). But if this cynicism comically reflects the superficiality of York's own recourse to his historical "right," or the callous lies with which his foes recast honest Gloucester's career as they accuse him before the king (III, i), it does not play into any larger consideration of the fictive reconstruction of history. Rather, the very transparency of Cade's lies or the retrospective falsehood of those who attack Gloucester sets off the implied truth of the few other historical accounts here (e.g., York's recital of his birthright, or even the pirate lieutenant's accusatory review of Suffolk's destructive career in 2, IV, i) which may be openly partisan but are not called into question factually as revisionism will be in later plays.

Again, the more significant fact about historical retrospect in these plays, rather than any particular cast given its few occurrences, is its relative absence. Prophecy and anticipation abound, as in the "hardly attained and hardly understood" oracles conjured up by the hapless duchess of Gloucester (2, I, iv), or

Gloucester's more lucid forevision of England's troubles at his downfall (2, III, i), or Elizabeth's false hopes for "Edward's off- spring in . . . [her] womb" (3, IV, iv, 18), or Henry's canny truths foretold about those future mighty opposites, Henry Richmond (3, IV, vi) and Richard Gloucester (3, V, vi), or Richard's own villainous plans (3, III, ii; V, vi). Such forevision, true and false, is a more telling presence here than remembrance of things past. Gloucester's image of a nation "undoing all as all had never been" is only an exaggeration of the essential truth about his England's neglect of its history. In the context of Part One, where Talbot had given such prominence to the idea of heroic renewal, its ab- sence here seems a severe loss. In their own right, however, Parts Two and Three do not call pointed attention to the loss of the past. They simply show us an England with little or no sense of its own heritage. One curious symptom of this national oblivion is the persistent recourse to classical and mythical models. With no evident consciousness of the Black Prince or Cordelion, no Arthur or "stout Pendragon" to inspire them, these embattled En- glishmen call on the whole lexicon of the ancients to characterize themselves. Margaret styles herself a Dido to Suffolk's bewitching Ascanius (2, III, ii, 114–118), and Suffolk places his death in line with Tully's, Caesar's, and Pompey's (2, IV, i, 136–139). Young Clifford will unite in himself that incongruous pair, Medea and Aeneas (2, V, ii, 58–65). Examples are ubiquitous, and none more wonderful, surely, than that of Henry sending Warwick off as his "Hector and . . . [his] Troy's true hope" while he remains in London with his "loving citizens" like "modest Dian circled with her nymphs" (3, IV, viii, 19–25). Such allusive fertility makes the lack of reference to English prototypes all the more remarkable.

Loss or simple lack, the neglect of their past is surely one among the failings of these nobles, who are "no good workmen" indeed. In a rare retrospect, Edward signals the end of Part Three by reviewing his bloody path to "England's royal throne," falsely interpreting this extirpation of Lancastrians as his "footstool of security" (3, V, vii, 1–14) and smugly oblivious of the deadly intentions Richard mutters aside to us. Even less than his ambitious father does Richard care for history and its claims, which oppress him as a "thorny wood" through which he will "hew . . . [his] way out with a bloody axe" (3, III, ii, 174–181). In his stance toward history and its authority, as in so many other respects, Richard is the nadir toward which this self-destructive English polity has been plummeting.

CHAPTER THREE

Richard III

"O, But Remember This Another Day"

If it played a minimal part in the second and third parts of *Henry VI*, memory floods the world of *Richard III* with peculiar force.[1] What is remembered not only affects the consciousness of the present; it is the perceived cause of current troubles, not in the sophisticated terms of political psychology with which a fallen Richard II will be able to predict Northumberland's defection from Bolingbroke and Pandulph can foresee John's murder of Arthur and its results, but in the simple and absolute terms of retributive justice with which the "high All-seer" here so plainly ordains that every wrongdoer gets exactly what is coming to him. One realization after another confirms the precise exactitude with which punishment is suited to the crime:

This is the day which in King Edward's time
I wished might fall on me when I was found
False to his children and his wife's allies;
This is the day wherein I wished to fall
By the false faith of him whom most I trusted;
This, this All-Souls' day to my fearful soul
Is the determined respite of my wrongs:
That high All-seer which I dallied with
Hath turned my feignèd prayer on my head
And given in earnest what I begged in jest.
Thus doth He force the swords of wicked men
To turn their own points in their masters' bosoms;
Thus Margaret's curse falls heavy on my neck:
"When he," quoth she, "shall split thy heart with sorrow,
Remember Margaret was a prophetess."—
Come lead me, officers, to the block of shame.
Wrong hath but wrong, and blame the due of blame.

                                             (V, i, 13–29)

The past actions to whose "determined respite" Buckingham
resigns himself here occur in the early stages of this play. And
though other memories are longer (notably those of Clarence, the
duchess of York, and Margaret), they extend, like Buckingham's,
only to "personal" history and thus to the horrors that Yorkists
and Lancastrians visited upon one another in the two preceding
plays. No more than in those plays do we hear of the Black Prince
or his father, and even Henry V is entirely forgotten. For all its
emphasis on the past, and for all the dominance that the past
holds over this play's dismal present, *Richard III* virtually inverts the ideal of "remembrance" embodied in Talbot. Dead victims rather than dead heroes live in memory here, and they haunt
the present rather than inspiring it. The funeral of the pathetic
Henry VI, that "poor key-cold figure of a holy king," is therefore as appropriate to the beginning of *Richard III* as his heroic

father's funeral had been to the opening of the first play in the series. And in one notable exception to the limited chronological reach of the pervasive retrospection, a trio of victims approaching their execution recalls the prototypical victim who serves as their model:

> O Pomfret, Pomfret! O thou bloody prison,
> Fatal and ominous to noble peers!
> Within the guilty closure of thy walls
> Richard the Second here was hacked to death.
> (III, iii, 9–12)

In this pattern, where continuity is maintained by retribution rather than renewal, the present victim customarily finds his precedent not in a renowned prototype (as the doomed lords do at Pomfret and as, in the corresponding pattern of renewal, the present hero does) but in his own prior victims, for whose "wrong" he now sees himself punished. He is, therefore, victim not only to another (most often, of course, to Richard) but to his own past deeds, as Buckingham realizes in the lines cited above. Clarence illustrates the common pattern even more vividly in the hellish nightmare that both foretells his own horrid punishment and recalls what "determined" it:

> Then came wand'ring by
> A shadow like an angel, with bright hair
> Dabbled in blood, and he shrieked out aloud,
> "Clarence is come—false, fleeting, perjured Clarence,
> That stabbed me in the field by Tewkesbury:
> Seize on him, Furies, take him unto torment!
> (I, iv, 52–57)

To speak thus of a "common pattern" is scarcely to impose a critical rage for order on this punctiliously designed play in which structural elements large and small, verbal and visual, are so symmetrically balanced. The striking fact for our topic is that the relationships between past and present are as neatly counterpointed, one deed or one death answering another, as are the antitheses Richard draws between himself and the sportive world in his opening speech, or the stichomythic dialogue of Richard and Anne in the second scene, or the alternating and opposite appearances of Richard and Richmond in the concluding sequences. The past recurs in the present with all the resounding quality of a direct echo—an effect achieved not only through such retrospective realizations as those of Clarence and Buckingham, but through the curses and lamentations of the women in the play as well. The Yorkist women feel the shock of each inevitable counterstroke more as the passive sufferers for their destructively active fathers, husbands, and sons than as former wrongdoers. Instead of the single moment of personal realization through remembrance as the pendulum swings back toward them (though Anne experiences such a moment in IV, i), the women tend to accumulate tally sheets of their painful losses by which the longer sufferer can claim a grim supremacy:

> *Queen Eliz*: Was never widow had so dear a loss.
> *Children*: Were never orphans had so dear a loss.
> *Duchess*: Was never mother had so dear a loss.
> Alas! I am the mother of these griefs:
> Their woes are parcelled, mine is general.
> She for an Edward weeps, and so do I;
> I for a Clarence weep, so doth not she:
> These babes for Clarence weep, and so do I;
> I for an Edward weep, so do not they.
> Alas, you three on me, threefold distressed,
> Pour all your tears! I am your sorrow's nurse,
> And I will pamper it with lamentation.
>
> (II, ii, 77–88)

Margaret later openly asserts the principle of seniority implicit in the duchess of York's lament:

If ancient sorrow be most reverent,
Give mine the benefit of seniory
And let my griefs frown on the upper hand.

(IV, iv, 35—37)

And if the duchess's age and station give her primacy among
doleful recollectors in the Yorkist circle ("Accursed and unquiet
wrangling days, / How many of you have mine eyes beheld" [II, iv,
55—56]), Margaret, her Lancastrian coeval, outsoars her in ven-
omous intensity.[2] Once a fierce participant in her own "right" and
now a lurking witness to the "tragedy" of Yorkist self-destruction
(IV, iv, 1—8), Margaret vindictively scores off the mortal debts paid
and still outstanding rather than merely bewailing her own losses:

> *Margaret*: I had an Edward, till a Richard killed him;
> I had a Harry, till a Richard killed him;
> Thou hadst an Edward, till a Richard killed him;
> Thou hadst a Richard, till a Richard killed him.
> *Duchess*: I had a Richard too, and thou didst kill him;
> I had a Rutland too, thou holp'st to kill him.
> .   .   .   .
> *Margaret*: Thy Edward he is dead, that killed my Edward;
> Thy other Edward dead, to quit my Edward;
> Young York he is but boot, because both they
> Matched not the high perfection of my loss.
> Thy Clarence he is dead that stabbed my Edward,
> And the beholders of this frantic play,
> Th'adulterate Hastings, Rivers, Vaughan, Grey,
> Untimely smoth'red in their dusky graves.
> Richard yet lives, hell's black intelligencer;
> Only reserved their factor to buy souls
> And send them thither. But at hand, at hand,
> Ensues his piteous and unpitied end.

(IV, iv, 40—74)

As in the genealogies that level heroes and failures to equivalent markers in a bloodline, Margaret's rigid account of these retributive scores strips most of these like-named lords of any ennobling or individualizing traits. Listing them thus emphasizes the evident helplessness of these various Edwards and Richards under the mechanical implacability of the force that makes "history" here primarily a matter of inescapable punishment for past actions— one's own or others'.[3]

The apparent (if not ultimate) exception to this common reduction is, of course, *the* Richard, who swells from his repeated citation as a mere item on the account sheet ("*a* Richard") to his proper abhorrent stature at its conclusion ("hell's black intelligencer") with his proper distinctive qualities ("that bottled spider, that foul bunch-backed toad" [81]) called into prominent verbal view. It is perfectly apt that he should both be reduced to one among the many echoed names on the list and be given his singular eminence over the others, for he is both contained within the larger pattern of retribution (hailed by Margaret, recognized by the several victimizers who become victims in their turn, and confirmed by the play's conclusion) and stands out in it as "himself alone." He stands out in every respect, of course, but in none more so than in the tremendous energy with which he opposes his own intense will against all other forces that might normally determine events. His efforts to shape the course of things according to his own designs have recently been most often described in terms (which the play certainly encourages) of theatrical art, with Richard as playwright, director, and star actor all in one.[4] In our context, however, those efforts are most notable for their necessary collision with the past and its legacy.

Like his assertion of personal will, Richard's stance toward history is a grotesque intensification of the attitude commonly shared by his contemporaries and immediate predecessors in the tetralogy. What had been in his father and others essential negligence of history's significance (Lucy's "sleeping neglection") becomes in him active opposition. Whereas they allowed the past to be "undone" through their selfish pursuits, he consciously sets out to undo it. This enterprise is, for our purposes, the crucial element in a makeup that is in every respect (except military prowess and the suscepti- bility to being called a "writhled shrimp") the absolute antithesis of Talbot's.

It is a doomed enterprise in any case, but Richard's ultimate failure to overcome the past is marked by a scornful disregard of it as an antagonist worthy of his best efforts. His keynote, as he steps forward to introduce his play, is "now." Though he must plan ahead in pitting himself against "the idle pleasures of these days," he has no more compelling vision of the future than he does of the past. His determination "to prove a villain" interests him even more than the particular goal to be reached thereby or any his- torical legacy he will undo (or might fulfill) in the process. As far as the latter is concerned, he alone refuses (or fails) to see in his own fall the retributive justice that is history's driving force in the play. But the early successes he enjoys involve adroit recastings of a past that, in its own right, holds no essential interest for him. With a spirit of deft knavery that differs as much from Margaret's straight lies about Gloucester on the one hand as it does from Cade's genealogical buffoonery on the other, Richard lures "simple plain Clarence" into a view of recent events that attributes all their evils to Queen Elizabeth and Mistress Shore.[5] And his early master- piece, the wooing and winning of Lady Anne, is undertaken with a jaunty confidence that he *can* simply "undo" the past:

> What though I killed her husband and her father?
> The readiest way to make the wench amends
> Is to become her husband and her father.
>
> (I, i, 154–156)

Then, after toying for a time with both Anne and the obvious truth ("Say that I slew them not?" [I, ii, 89]), Richard finally trig- gers her astonishing reversal by both insisting on that truth ("for

I did kill King Henry"; "'twas I that stabbed young Edward" [179–181]) and persuading the baffled widow that *she* was its ultimate cause: "But 'twas thy heavenly face that set me on" (182). As Richard himself points out when he shares his own elation with us after his stunning conquest, for Anne to believe and invest in this "hidden" motive and its radical reinterpretation of the past is equivalent to forgetting the plain facts:

> Ha!
> Hath she forgot already that brave prince,
> Edward, her lord, whom I, some three months since,
> Stabbed in my angry mood at Tewkesbury?
>
> (238–241)

Forgetting, however, is the rarer action in *Richard III*, especially when no such sudden rush of ego-gratification as the one Richard sets loose here in the hapless Anne comes into play. Remembering, rather, is the norm, and where Richard's former deeds are concerned, Margaret is memory's most insistent voice: "Out, devil! I do remember them too well" (I, iii, 117). Nor does Richard maintain his early momentum in his assaults on such memories. Never again does he throw himself into "undoing" the past with the gusto that inspired his playacting for Anne, and his later offhanded or lackluster efforts in this regard betray more arrogant contempt for history than vigorous hostility toward it. For him, to a degree even Lady Macbeth at her strongest could only envy, "what's done is done."

Perhaps for that reason, Richard meets his first real frustrations when he counts too easily on others' capacity to disregard both the plain truth and the painful experience of the past. When Buckingham faithfully delivers to the citizenry Richard's outrageous "historical" claim to the throne, wherein his "lineaments, / Being the right idea of . . . [his] father / Both in . . . form and nobleness of mind," are cited as proof of his legitimacy and Edward's bastardy, even that customarily pliant audience "spake not a word, /

But, like dumb statuës or breathing stones, / Stared each on other, and looked deadly pale" (III, v, 71–92; vii, 3–26). As the moralizing scrivener asks with respect to the fabricated indictment of Hastings, "Who is so gross / That cannot see this palpable device?" (III, vi, 10–11). Richard has the means to enforce his way over the balking citizens whether they believe his hastily revamped history (and his coyly played "maid's part") or not. But his subsequent attempt to undo Elizabeth's memory is more painfully outrageous and (if we judge by her subsequent action) even less successful than the facile historical fiction he tosses off for the mob. Richard does not even try to rewrite the past for the woman whose brother and children he has murdered. He simply asks her to forget it, to "drown the sad remembrance of these wrongs" in the Lethe of her soul. What he offers her to aid such drowning is his own grotesque version of "renewal," as opposite to Talbot's ideal of renewal as it can be, since it depends on forgetting the dead victims who will be replaced rather than reviving the dead hero in his living remembrancer:

> *Richard*: If I did take the kingdom from your sons,
> To make amends I'll give it to your daughter;
> If I have killed the issue of your womb,
> To quicken your increase I will beget
> Mine issue of your blood upon your daughter.
>   .   .   .   .
> *Elizabeth*: Yet thou didst kill my children.
> *Richard*: But in your daughter's womb I bury them,
> Where, in that nest of spicery, they will breed
> Selves of themselves, to your recomforture.
>   (IV, iv, 294–298, 422–425)

Though Elizabeth ends their long set-to by apparently opting for this callous and unsavory renewal through oblivion ("Shall I forget myself to be myself?" [420]), she has, throughout, harped on the very string that Richard would undo—the past—and rightly insisted that he cannot simply sever what will be from what has been, that his future is already fixed in the sorrowful shape his former deeds have given it:

> *Elizabeth*: What canst thou swear by now?
> *Richard*: The time to come.
> *Elizabeth*: That thou hast wrongèd in the time o'erpast;
> For I myself have many tears to wash
> Hereafter time, for time past wronged by thee.
> The children live whose fathers thou hast slaughtered,
> Ungoverned youth, to wail it in their age;
> The parents live whose children thou hast butchered,
> Old barren plants, to wail it with their age.
> Swear not by time to come, for that thou hast
> Misused ere used, by times ill-used o'erpast.
>
> (IV, iv, 387–396)

Whatever Richard may think about his apparent (and in any case short-lived) triumph over Elizabeth and her "sad remembrance" here, his match against the past proves to be no real contest.[6] If he has shown arrogant symptoms of not taking this struggle or this opponent seriously enough, of not using his most creative energy to drown or deceive memory, we see that in fact not even his vicious "best" ever stood a chance here, that the providential dice have been loaded against any such effort all along. Despite his last stand, there *is* no hazard in the cast upon which he sets his life.

The inevitable turn in memory's favor is signalled even before Elizabeth stymies Richard's second venture as "a jolly thriving wooer." It occurs when he first appears wearing his uneasy crown. The fatal name of Richmond begins to sound insistently here, and for the first time we are allowed to look inside a fretful Richard and see him chafing at a memory he cannot stifle:

> I do remember me Henry the Sixth
> Did prophesy that Richmond should be king

When Richmond was a little peevish boy.
A king!—perhaps—perhaps—

(IV, ii, 94-97)

His internal recollection, even less able than his facile fiction about Edward's birth, can only oppose futile skeptical sneers against the unalterable facts of what did and did not happen, what was and was not said: "How chance the prophet could not at that time / Have told me, I being by, that I should kill him?" (99–100).[7] Like his old antagonist, Margaret, Richard now remembers too well. The prophecy is one of those firm cords, too intrinse for Richard to unloose, binding the present and future to the past.

The past he cannot undo comes back to haunt Richard most expressly and oppressively, of course, on Bosworth eve. In a sequence that is unique in the histories and that epitomizes this play's memorialization of dead victims rather than dead heroes, the ghosts of those Richard has destroyed "revive" to destroy him with their echoing refrain, heaping the burden of the past on his bunched back: "To-morrow in the battle think on me, / And fall thy edgeless sword: despair, and die!" (V, iii, 135–136). As Elizabeth had pointed out to him, as Margaret had exultantly proclaimed, and as every emphatically punctuated instance of retribution in the play makes clear, Richard's past has "determined" (in Buckingham's accurate term) his end. And the past catches up with him at Bosworth Field.

There is, however, for all its validity and for all the vivid onstage presence of the ghosts who embody it, something abstract and incomplete about this last statement. It is *Richmond* who defeats and kills Richard at Bosworth. And what is curious about this fact in the context I have been developing here is Richmond's own comparative "neglection" of the "times . . . o'erpast" that recur so potently for every other principal in the play. If Richard opposes and is finally whelmed by the past, Richmond, his nemesis, neither embodies nor consciously revives any positive historical force. True, all those dead victims who curse Richard also confer their blessing on Richmond (Henry as prophet and ghost, the others as ghosts) and dub him the "offspring of the house of Lancaster" (V, iii, 137). And he does, in his final speech, briefly sum up the "dire division" of York and Lancaster that his marriage with Elizabeth will heal. But otherwise, he scarcely looks back at all. His only voiced "remembrance" is of his "fair dream" on the eve of Bosworth itself. In every other respect, and through every theatrical device, he is made Richard's exact antithesis, calling on God and right and companionship and love and union and the fruitful "harvest of perpetual peace" (V, ii, 15). If Richard would undo the past, however, Richmond does little to revive it and nothing to "awake remembrance" of the "valiant dead" in his own person. Perhaps his detachment from the bloodstained entanglements of recent history best qualifies him as victorious peacemaker.[8] In any case, for all his emphasis on liberation and union, he never speaks of restoration and never evokes those heroic predecessors who are (or could be) as much *his* heritage as that of any noble Englishman. Oddly, the only allusion to "our fathers" whose victories are celebrated "in record" is Richard's own at Bosworth's zero hour (V, iii, 333–336).

It would be neater for my thesis, neater for the tetralogy, and neater even for this exceptionally neat play itself if it were otherwise—if Richmond rose phoenixlike from Talbot's ashes, bringing back to life all that earlier hero's ideals of historic renewal through emulation. But it is not so, and it would be a feeble (if not unprecedented) absurdity to fault Shakespeare for not properly filling out my pattern (or my intimation of his pattern) more symmetrically. For whatever reasons, Richmond is given more forevision binding "the time to come" that is the Elizabethan audience's present to his own establishment of Tudor harmony than he is the sort of retrospect that would deepen the Elizabethan heritage through him into England's longer heroic past. And the tetralogy that started with such a positive representation of historic renewal never shows the full recovery of that ideal, though the loss of memory that so largely besets England in the middle two plays is "corrected" by the retributive force with which the past swings back upon the present in *Richard III*. This resurgence of memory, focused on past wrongs, is a painful one for an England that still seems to have forgotten its better self. Richmond offers the nation a new start, but not much sense of renewal.

Contained within the play, if not in its celebrative conclusion, are suggestions of what such a sense might entail. Buckingham, still begging in jest what ought to be given in earnest, publicly "persuades" Richard to save the realm and its true heritage:

> The noble isle doth want her proper limbs;
> Her face defaced with scars of infamy,
> Her royal stock graft with ignoble plants,
> And almost should'red in the swallowing gulf
> Of dark forgetfulness and deep oblivion.
> Which to recure, we heartily solicit
> Your gracious self to take on you the charge
> And kingly government of this your land.
>
> (III, vii, 125–132)

That "swallowing gulf / Of dark forgetfulness and deep oblivion," however lightly Buckingham himself may call up its image, is precisely the horror an earlier Gloucester had seen "undoing all as all had never been" in his time. Richard, of course, would scarcely "recure" it, since it suits his purpose to foster "dark forgetfulness" and thwart remembrance. And Richmond, for all his other virtues, shows little interest in recovering the past from "deep oblivion." Richard's true opposite in this regard is not Richmond but young Edward V, who alone in this play lends his clear (if small) voice to the ideal of keeping the heroic past alive. Edward fills the dramatic interim while his puckish brother is being fetched from sanctuary in III, i, by reflecting on the vitality of heroic fame and on Caesar's double claim to it as both hero and historian:

Prince: I do not like the Tower, of any place.
Did Julius Caesar build that place, my lord?
Buckingham: He did, my gracious lord, begin that place,
Which, since, succeeding ages have re-edified.
Prince: Is it upon record, or else reported
Successively from age to age, he built it?
Buckingham: Upon record, my gracious lord.
Prince: But say, my lord, it were not regist'red,
Methinks the truth should live from age to age,
As 'twere retailed to all posterity,
Even to the general all-ending day.

.   .   .   .

That Julius Caesar was a famous man:
With what his valor did enrich his wit,
His wit set down to make his valor live.
Death makes no conquest of this conqueror,
For now he lives in fame, though not in life.

(III, i, 68–88)

And then the young prince promises (though with a fatally ominous conditional clause) to renew in his own person his heroic English forebears:

An if I live until I be a man,
I'll win our ancient right in France again
Or die a soldier as I lived a king.

(91–93)

Richard, who has been muttering dark threats aside all this while, will snuff out this "forward spring" before its promise can mature. One could say, however, that the play (if not any hero in the play) upholds the prince's ideal, passing on his living truth "from age to age" and defeating Richard's attempt to smother that truth along with the prince in "deep oblivion."[9]

Such a claim would, of course, loudly beg a question that this play and this tetralogy do not probe—namely, the actual truth of the history being represented. However clearly we may see the contours of the Tudor myth in Shakespeare's crooked Richard and straight Richmond, the play, like the three that precede it, does not call its own historical authenticity into question. Though he has such shallow grounding in the remembered past and there-fore may seem all the more a *deus ex machina*, Richmond is no more exposed as "too good to be true" in this play's world than Talbot was in his. The heroes of the Hundred Years War may be forgotten in *Richard III*, but nothing suggests that they were of an idealized stature that could no longer be realized in the play's dismal present. Prince Edward's promise may be cut short, but it is not undercut.[10]

When the second tetralogy ends, the idea of heroic renewal will have been realized again as it is not realized here by the virtually rootless Richmond. In this respect, as in others, Henry V is a more mighty opposite to Richard than the nemesis who kills and succeeds him. But if Henry thus fulfills the promise that young Edward barely has time to utter here, it is with a far more com-plex sense of it and of the historical "truth" that should live from age to age.

CHAPTER FOUR

King John

"Perfect Richard" versus "This Old World"

King John, that "singular" play among Shakespeare's histories of the nineties, is commonly seen to be transitional between the two tetralogies from which its narrative stands chronologically apart. Its departure from the earlier series and anticipation of the second one is usually perceived in the tough-minded realism of its dramatized political dilemmas.[1] And in no respect can both its transitional and its singular status be seen more distinctly than in the way that realism is enforced through this play's recollection and renewal of the "valiant dead." According to William Matchett, "the memory of Coeur-de-lion haunts this play as the mythically heightened image of a good and heroic king."[2] So, it might be said, did the memory of Henry V haunt *1 Henry VI* ("Henry the Fifth, thy ghost I invocate" [I, i, 52]), and so will memories of his father and grandfather haunt Richard II's play (if not his own consciousness). But the distinctive nature of the remembered hero's presence in *King John* forces the very questions about the viable truth and effective use of the remembered past that were left unasked by the first tetralogy and that will become increasingly a concern of the second. For nowhere else in the histories is a lost leader so vividly renewed as Cordelion is here in the nonhistorical characterization of his illegitimate son, the jaunty Bastard Faulconbridge. And this fictive character's unique role in *John*'s dramatized history highlights the disconcerting problems which this play exposes but does not resolve.[3]

Though the problematic nature of the present political situation in *John* depends implicitly on recent history, there is relatively little retrospective argument in the play. What *is* at issue is seldom posed in terms of what *has* happened. It may seem natural that our sense of this play's concerns depends less on prior events than is the case with the six plays that are "sequels" in the two tetralogies and with whose antecedents we are therefore presumably familiar. But in fact, both tetralogies' lead-off plays ground their current problems more fully in retrospective controversies than *John* does. Nothing like Mortimer's lengthy genealogical survey for the benefit of his eager heir in *1 Henry VI* occurs here. And only the briefest flurries in *John* anticipate the prolonged disputes over past events that embroil Richard's polity in the first scene and Henry's at its very inception in *Richard II*. When the wearer of the English crown and the young claimant to it meet before Angiers in Act II of *John*, King Philip of France gives an account of Arthur's legal right that contrasts sharply in both its clarity and its brevity with the Yorkist rehearsals of genealogy in *1 and 2 Henry VI*:

> Geoffrey was thy elder brother born,
> And this his son. England was Geoffrey's right
> And this is Geoffrey's in the name of God.

How comes it then that thou art called a king,
When living blood doth in these temples beat,
Which owe the crown that thou o'ermasterest?

(II, i, 104–109)

John doesn't even attempt to answer this question but merely deflects it by asking what business it is of France's. And what could be made the basis of a serious argument on constitutional historical grounds—Richard I's will bequeathing the crown to John—is relegated to one brief assertion that rebounds in Elinor's face through Constance's almost inevitable play on words:

> *Elinor*: I can produce
> A will that bars the title of thy son.
> *Constance*: Ay, who doubts that? A will! A wicked will;
> A woman's will; a cankered grandam's will!
>
> (191–194)

Elinor had, in fact, already privately conceded the issue of legal right in a "whispered" aside to her son in the play's opening sequence:

> *John*: Our strong possession and our right for us.
> *Elinor*: Your strong possession much more than your right,
> Or else it must go wrong with you and me.
>
> (I, i, 39–40)

As far as the play is concerned, then, the issue of legal heritage is in and of itself a clear and simple one favoring Arthur, and no one debates it with the kind of conflicting historical claims that lend more heat than light to disputes in other histories.

But the clarity of this issue, rather than providing a firm basis for the right view of the conflict between John and Arthur, only intensifies the problematic nature of "right" in that conflict as the play presents it. For, as the Faulconbridge case that dominates the play's first act shows so pointedly, legal right may be at odds with actual right. After the brief opening sequence has expeditiously introduced Arthur's (or his supporters') challenge to John's "borrowed majesty," the Faulconbridge brothers are ushered into court and the case of the elder's legitimacy is set before John as judge. Robert, the younger, exhibits his incapacity to thrive in this play's tough world not only by his spindly shape and the difficulty he has getting a word in edgewise but by the simple faith on which he stands when he finally does find his voice: "But truth is truth" (I, i, 105). For one thing, that tame tautology is oblivious to the two very different meanings of truth (or true) that are already becoming crucial to our understanding of the situation. Robert means truth as fact—what is, is. When the Bastard shortly thereafter acknowledges Elinor as his grandmother "by chance but not by truth" (169), however, the word takes on a different (and in this case opposite) meaning of "right." As Cordelion's illegitimate son, he is not truly (or rightly) Elinor's grandson, even though he truly (or actually) is so. The French ambassador had already introduced this alternative meaning of "true" into the play's opening lines when he spoke of Arthur's "right and true" claim to the throne, using the two adjectives as synonyms. Poor Robert's apparent "truism" is ambiguous, then, in a way he scarcely comprehends and proves doubly hopeless when John points out that in this case neither sort of truth matters here in the eyes of the law. Though Robert would seem to have both the facts and the right of the matter on his side, the law ignores both: since Lady Faulconbridge was married when she bore the brash Bastard, he is legally legitimate, willy-nilly.

The play thus swiftly alerts us to basic problems that are its concern—problems that first emerge here through gaps between right and truth (or between the two meanings of "true") and between what the law sanctions and what we plainly see to be both "right and true." No one can miss the relevance of the Faulconbridge case to the central crisis of the realm, where Arthur's patent legal right collides not only with the actuality of the crowned John but with our perception that this helpless boy seems unsuited for the role of king. Whereas his "powerless hand" welcomes the foreign support of France and the blustering slayer of Cordelion, "English John" shows early on a good deal of what the Bastard calls the "mettle of a king" (II, i, 15, 10, 401). Thus focused, the problem is one of kingship, of determining who the "true" king is, and for a time the audience is very much in the position of the citizens of Angiers, who "stand securely on their battlements / As in a theatre" and watch "the undetermined differences of kings" as the contestants for that title square off: "He that proves the king, / To him will we prove loyal" (II, i, 374–375, 355, 270–271). Even focused thus in political terms, the problem is progressively compounded rather than resolved for us, as John's kingly "mettle" disintegrates through the very process of eliminating Arthur and the legal "right" embodied in him. But the play extends its questions about the "right and true" beyond the immediate political issue, where the presumably natural conjunction between these two terms breaks down. Largely through the Bastard's distinctive role, *King John* tugs at some of the unexamined premises underlying the bright historical faith of a Prince Edward (in *Richard III*) that "the truth should live from age to age" and of a Lucy (in *1 Henry VI*) that the true hero of the past can be revived, phoenixlike and undiminished, to bear his nation's standard in a new age.[4]

From his first entrance, the Bastard's cavalier, cocksure manner wins the approval of his audience onstage ("I like thee well" [I, i, 148]) and off and gains a firm hold on our view of the action. That hold is strengthened by what we quickly sense to be the Bastard's natural affinity for both the right and the true. His outspoken insistence on describing things just as they are breaks the decorum and bares the truth in public scenes from the very opening. And when he is given the advantage of a private soliloquy to confide in us (a privilege that is almost exclusively his in the play), he does so with biting candor, whether he mocks the customary ways of "new-made honor" (as in I, i) or rails at a world given over to commodity (as in II, i). At the same time, the Bastard shows a solid sense of right-mindedness that is readily distinguishable from mere law. He "wins" the dispute with his brother in our eyes, after all, by *not* accepting the patently wrong legal victory John offers him and by affirming instead what we plainly see to be the "right" of the matter: that Robert is the true son of old Faulconbridge, and that the Bastard himself is "perfect Richard." His cheerful willingness to forfeit "many and many a foot of land" for the "honor" of his Plantagenet heritage (164, 183) gives earnest that this Bastard will prove more "right and true" than those who make such strenuous claims for their own legitimacy: "Well won is still well shot, / And I am I, howe'er I was begot" (174–175). If *this* is "but a bastard to the time" (207), then we may already suspect what events will prove so surely and so sorely: that the *time* is out of joint.[5]

Throughout the play, in fact, the Bastard exposes the imperfections of the world around him in two complementary ways: as a commentator on them and as an exemplary contrast to them. As the problem of right and true action—and of determining the truth itself—grows more tortuous in the last two acts, the Bastard's exemplary role takes on more weight and more sober implications. In the earlier action in France, as the two sides vie to "prove" who is king of England, the Bastard is primarily a commentator. Though his exchanges with Austria initiate the first phase of his hero's role, his major function on the battlefield is to provide a solid voice for the actual state of affairs when rhetorical claims of "right" on both sides tend to float free from it:

John: Doth not the crown of England prove the king?
And if not that, I bring you witnesses,
Twice fifteen thousand hearts of England's breed—
Bastard: Bastards, and else.

.   .   .   .

Philip: As many and as well-born bloods as those—
Bastard: Some bastards, too.
Philip: Stand in his face to contradict his claim.

(II, i, 273–280)

This sort of plain truth, which the Bastard interjects among the airy orations, gratifies our sense of reality while right remains problematic. Instead of simply lending his lion-hearted presence in support of John's cause (as his *Troublesome Raigne* counterpart does), Shakespeare's Richard maintains something of an observer's detachment and calls the shots as we see them.

He does so, however, with less sardonic humor and more direct outrage when the leaders of both sides opt for the Citizen's skin-saving compromise—when they choose, that is, a hastily contrived marriage between John's niece Blanche and the Dauphin Lewis over the Bastard's own lusty Plantagenet suggestion that the warriors join forces to lay the frustrating town flat and *then* resume their fight over the royal title to it and to England. Up to this point, however perplexed the issue, the two kings have apparently led their respective sides of it with what the Bastard recognized as royal "mettle." But now even that standard is hypocritically forsaken:

Mad world! Mad kings! Mad composition!
John, to stop Arthur's title in the whole,
Hath willingly departed with a part,
And France, whose armor conscience buckled on,
Whom zeal and charity brought to the field
As God's own soldier, rounded in the ear
With that same purpose-changer, that sly devil,
That broker, that still breaks the pate of faith,
That daily break-vow, he that wins of all,
Of kings, of beggars, old men, young men, maids,
Who, having no external thing to lose
But the word "maid," cheats the poor maid of that,

That smooth-faced gentleman, tickling commodity,
Commodity, the bias of the world.

$$(561-574)$$

So much for whatever right either side had claimed heretofore. And the actuality which both would nonetheless still hide under the cover of high-sounding terms is laid bare by the Bastard's vivid personification of "that smooth-faced gentleman, tickling commodity." The Bastard's own credit with us as a touchstone of things-as-they-are is maintained by his frank acknowledgment that the cause of his erstwhile enemy France, just abandoned at commodity's urging, had been a noble one and by his willingness to turn his scathing irony on himself—perhaps doing himself less than justice in the process, if we think back to his easy release of many a foot of land: "And why rail I on this commodity? / But for because he hath not wooed me yet" (587–588). His final bitter resolution to follow the sordid royal example ("Gain, be my lord, for I will worship thee!") may mislead us to suppose for the moment that he, too, is forsaking truth-as-right.[6] He ends Act II, however, as the exclusive and outspoken expositor of truth-as-fact, and we are bound to share the accurate view he offers of the play's world at this point.

That view involves a strongly felt attitude, of course, as well as an accurate analysis. A world (or a king) that turns according to the bias of commodity is, as the Bastard sees it, "mad." But as seen by the papal legate Pandulph, who now arrives on the scene to break up the newly formed league between England and France, such a world is merely (and familiarly) "old." When John musters enough heroic spirit to defy him, Pandulph, the very patron saint of commodity, uses a compound of casuistry and intimidation to persuade France to break "the deep-sworn faith, peace, amity, [and] true love" to England with which that slippery-conscienced king had just broken his former deep-sworn faith, peace, amity, and true love to Constance (III, 1, 224–320). And when John wins the ensuing battle, Pandulph offers the distraught dauphin, Lewis, the consolations of his worldly wise philosophy. "How green you are and fresh in this old world," he observes as he explains the hard law of realpolitik by which the newly victorious John will inevitably do away with Arthur to secure himself and will just as inevitably alienate his subjects and thereby make himself insecure in the process:

> A sceptre snatched with an unruly hand
> Must be as boisterously maintained as gained,
> And he that stands upon a slippery place
> Makes nice of no vile hold to stay him up.
> That John may stand, then Arthur needs must fall;
> So be it, for it cannot be but so.
>
> .   .   .   .
>
> This act so evilly borne shall cool the hearts
> Of all his people and freeze up their zeal,
> That none so small advantage shall step forth
> To check his reign, but they will cherish it.
>
> (III, iv, 135–152)

Far from being a cause for dismay or a sign of madness, the fact that "this old world" turns according to such surely predictable biases ("so be it, for it cannot be but so") amply gratifies Pandulph's cynical political science, which can work its own clear-eyed advantages out of others' confusion: "'Tis wonderful / What may be wrought out of their discontent" (178–179). And so he prompts Lewis's invasion of John's troubled England.

However unsavory Pandulph's way of conducting his holy mission may seem, we must credit the accuracy of his vision, for in a marvellously chilling sequence of the preceding scene we have just watched John insinuate his way toward the deadly command that (as Pandulph predicts) must mark the fatal turning point in his career:

John: Good Hubert! Hubert, Hubert, throw thine eye
On yon young boy. I'll tell thee what, my friend,
He is a very serpent in my way,
And wheresoe'er this foot of mine doth tread
He lies before me. Dost thou understand me?
Thou art his keeper.
Hubert: And I'll keep him so
That he shall not offend your majesty.
John: Death.
Hubert: My lord?
John: A grave.
Hubert: He shall not live.
John: Enough.

                                        (III, iii, 59–66)

What John does here is all the more appalling—and seems all the
more true to whatever knowledge of the world we may share,
willingly or not, with Pandulph—because it is not out-and-out
villainy of Richard III's gleeful sort but a descent into evil under
the evident compulsion of political necessity as the papal legate
spells it out.[7] And through this transitional mid-section of the
play, while the Bastard is off on an errand that suits his jaunty
irreverence (shaking "the bags of hoarding abbots" and setting
free "their imprisoned angels" [III, iii, 7–9]), the legate's cool
analysis replaces Richard's lively voice as our primary guide to the
true state of affairs, to things as they are rather than as we might
prefer them to be. As we watch the world according to Pandulph,
we see history as bitter truth, not as an inspiring model of the
"right and true."

When the Bastard reports back to John in Act IV, the problem
of truth and of any "right and true" understanding of it or response to it is taking on a new dimension that can baffle even
Pandulph's confident cynicism. Everyone can see that the actual
state of affairs in England is worsening, but no one can any longer

see that actuality so clearly as some still believe they do and as Pandulph always makes it his business to do. The crux here is the death of Arthur. Would Pandulph suppose that "in this iron age" a hireling such as Hubert would risk his own neck and forsake "the wealth of all the world" to spare the boy out of mere feelings of mercy and love (IV, i, 60, 131)? In any case, the ground for sure knowledge of the full truth disappears when Arthur, seen by no one but us, leaps to his death from his prison walls. By doing so, he foils John's plan to appease the "angry lords" who, following Pandulph's cynically prophetic script to the letter, are turning the supposed murder of Arthur into a cause for rebellion. But he also subverts such suppositions themselves. Lacking our privileged view of Arthur's fall, the lords who arrive on the scene and the Bastard who follows them can only speculate on what actually happened and base their options for "right" action on their consequent assumptions.

Even knowing what we know, what *is* the truth about Arthur's death and about John's or Hubert's guilt or innocence with respect to it? They did not, of course, actually kill him, but to what extent are they nonetheless responsible? More free, perhaps, in their relative ignorance to reach absolute conclusions than we are, the lords quickly judge it a murder and then put the tough question to the Bastard: "Sir Richard, what think you?" (IV, iii, 41). The actual difficulty of providing a valid answer is further exposed when Hubert rushes in with his untimely report that "Arthur doth live" (75). When the lords threaten to punish him on the spot as a "murderer," Hubert protests his innocence in terms that recall the "innocent" Robert Faulconbridge, who thought that truth was truth:

> Do not prove me so.
> Yet I am none. Whose tongue soe'er speaks false,
> Not truly speaks; who speaks not truly, lies.
>
> (90–92)

Hubert himself has just disproved the over-simplified logic of that defense by speaking falsely (Arthur does not live) without lying (he supposed he spoke the truth). And his claim of innocence (false in its reasoning, true—but *how* true?—in fact) only emphasizes the difficulty of speaking truly as things now stand. "The truth *should* live from age to age," yes. But this sequence exposes more pointedly than anything in the preceding histories the problems inherent in determining, maintaining, and recovering the truth and thus in authenticating history itself (though it does so in a context that *feels* more true than *Richard III* does, as we have seen, precisely because it does not present its world and its villains and heroes with such sure clarity).[8]

From this point on in *King John*, virtually everyone loses his way (and not least the critical reader looking for the neatly coherent denouement of a well-made play). Even Pandulph, whose non-nervous system makes him so much less vulnerable than others to the shocks of moral or emotional turmoil, fails to keep his firm grip on things. After John furthers his own moral and emotional collapse by submitting to the papal legate he once so boldly defied, Lewis derails Pandulph's over-confident attempt to "hush again this storm of war" (V, i, 20). We could say that Pandulph fails his own creed rather than the reverse in this instance, since his commodity-ruled norms of political calculations should have foreseen that Lewis, who now holds "the best cards for the game / To win this easy match played for a crown" (V, ii, 105–106), would defy the legate's order to cease and desist. But in fact, as we might already infer from the perplexed instance of Arthur's death, neither Pandulph nor his upstart protégé can see *all* the cards—can take into account, for example, the winds and tides amidst which ignorant armies clash by night in *King John*'s final act. Like other courses, that of realpolitik, placing its faith in hard facts and cold calculation, proves error-prone as the action of the play disintegrates toward its conclusion.[9]

Among the other possible courses, the Bastard and the English lords choose opposite ones, and that taken by the lords no doubt appears to us the more faulty from its very beginning. We know they are over-hasty and over-certain in their judgment on Arthur's death, and we can scarcely consider Lewis a much happier choice for the English throne than the crumbling John. But Shakespeare makes our own judgment more problematic than does the author of *The Troublesome Raigne*. In that play we are forewarned of Lewis's treacherous "French" plan to dispose of his English supporters once they have served his nasty purpose. In *John*, however, we are left as ignorant as the lords on this point for the time being and are forced to participate with them to this extent in the difficulty of choosing rightly. Certainly they have ample cause for their disaffection from John, however shaky their judgment about the "murder" may be. And if Salisbury approximates Pandulph's casuistry as he later rationalizes his decision, he does not evidently do so willingly or happily:

> But such is the infection of the time
> That, for the health and physic of our right,
> We cannot deal but with the very hand
> Of stern injustice and confusèd wrong.
>
> (V, ii, 20–23)

I see no reason to doubt the sincerity of his futile wish for a better world in which truer courses of action would be clear and sure:

> O nation, that thou couldst remove!
> That Neptune's arms, who clippeth thee about,
> Would bear thee from the knowledge of thyself,
> And grapple thee unto a pagan shore,
> Where these two Christian armies might combine
> The blood of malice in a vein of league,
> And not to spend it so unneighborly! [10]
>
> (33–39)

What I would emphasize about this image of the English as heroic crusaders assaulting the pagan foe "in stronds afar remote" is that it is explicitly *opposed* to the unhappy reality of English history as we see it and as the lords are experiencing it here. Though it might well call to our minds the figure of Cordelion (on whose important presence in and behind the play I will focus shortly), Salisbury does not overtly evoke a "true" historical model of heroic action to inspire emulation. Rather, darkening our ironic awareness that he actually knows less than he supposes, Salisbury wishes that the English knew nothing of their actual condition at all. The premises of heroic renewal that found their active embodiment in Talbot and their hopeful voice in young Edward's assertion that "the truth should live from age to age" are thus overturned by Salisbury, who places such heroic endeavors in the realm of fantasy rather than history. His fervent wish to escape from the reality that oppresses him into an imagined world of glorious crusades will be echoed by that increasingly weary realist, Henry Bolingbroke.

The Bastard, too, keeps the gap between fictive heroes and sordid reality visible for us through the play's concluding scenes, but he does so in a positive and creative way that has more vital appeal than Salisbury's anguished wishful thinking and that anticipates Bolingbroke's inventive son more than that king so wan with care. What impresses us first about the Bastard's response to the "vast confusion" signalled by Arthur's death is that, unlike those who suppose they *know*, he openly acknowledges that he is lost and articulates what we see to be the plain truth that the plain truth is nowhere to be found:

> I am amazed, methinks, and lose my way
> Among the thorns and dangers of this world.
> .   .   .   .
> From forth this morsel of dead royalty
> The life, the right and truth of all this realm

Is fled to heaven, and England now is left
To tug and scamble and to part by th'teeth
The unowed interest of proud swelling state.

.   .   .   .

Now powers from home and discontents at home
Meet in one line, and vast confusion waits,
As doth a raven on a sick-fallen beast,
The imminent decay of wrested pomp.
Now happy he whose cloak and ceinture can
Hold out this tempest.

(IV, iii, 140–156)

The soliloquy that ended Act II had expressed the Bastard's
recognition of the evident truth that right was overswayed by
commodity and suggested in the process (despite his disgusted
profession of allegiance to "Gain") his sense of detachment from
such a "mad world." Now that both truth and right have "fled"
and are not only disregarded but indeterminable, he does not de-
tach himself from "the thorns and dangers of this world" or pull
his "cloak and ceinture" about him to "hold out this tempest."
Rather, he commits himself to decisive action:

I'll to the king.
A thousand businesses are brief in hand,
And heaven itself doth frown upon the land.

(157–159)

This sudden decision and his consequent action do not follow in
any logical or rational way from the terms in which the Bastard
has just described the world that amazes him. As those terms indicate, his decision here *must* be an existential one, choosing a
way despite his own awareness that whatever "rightness" he in-
vests it with is not inherent in it.[11]

From this point on, Richard's effort is largely a creative one.[12] If
truth and right are nowhere to be found, he will invent them where
they *should* be, in the crowned person of the king, and will act (in

both senses now) as though they were actually there. He first tries to instill into the drooping John himself the lion-heartedness proper to royalty:

> Be great in act, as you have been in thought.
> Let not the world see fear and sad distrust
> Govern the motion of a kingly eye.
> Be stirring as the time; be fire with fire.
>
> .   .   .   .
>
> Away, and glister like the god of war
> When he intendeth to become the field.
> Show boldness and aspiring confidence.
>
> (V, i, 45–56)

When the best response John can muster is to turn "the ordering of the present time" over to the Bastard himself, Richard sets about that Herculean task by acting and speaking for a king he now knows to be a fiction of his own making:

> Now hear our English king,
> For thus his royalty doth speak in me.
>
> .   .   .   .
>
> Know the gallant monarch is in arms,
> And like an eagle o'er his aery towers,
> To souse annoyance that comes near his nest.
>
> (V, ii, 128–150)

And when these brave words meet defiance from Lewis and the rebel lords, the Bastard actually dismisses John (whose "heart is sick," not lionish [V, iii, 4]) from the field and carries on in his stead: "That misbegotten devil, Faulconbridge, / In spite of spite, alone upholds the day" (V, iv, 4–5).

In spite of spite—and in spite of the awareness Richard shares with us that neither the right nor "the gallant monarch" he "alone upholds" have any firm foundation. And at one level we must also be aware that, for all his heroics, the Bastard cannot provide a romance's conclusion for this play's story. He cannot change history by repulsing the French and saving the kingdom for the majestic "John" he is determined to create. The presentation does not overtly prod our awareness of this impossibility, but of course a fictive victory of this sort would do so by jarring against our sense of the truth, our understanding of what is and is not dramatically acceptable in the play's own historical terms. In fact, like Salisbury's fantasy of a happily crusading England, the Bastard's fictive evocation of a heroic King John serves to validate by contrast the play's commitment to the harder truths of the history it dramatizes.

In ways that distinguish it, then, from the first tetralogy, *King John* touches and teases the problem of its own historical authenticity and historical fiction.[13] Most significant for our topic is the way in which it does so through the Bastard's kinship with Cordelion. As we have seen, the play includes little retrospective controversy that would provide a historical backdrop for the "vast confusion" of its present action. Instead, allusions to the past mostly involve the heroic figure of Cordelion, who provides a pervasive and ever-widening contrast to the ways of "this old world" in general and to the increasingly wretched John in particular. The grand image of Cordelion is not, of course, dependent here on verbal allusions alone, for it is visibly present throughout the play in the person of the Bastard.[14]

That the Bastard is identified absolutely with his heroic father is one of the clear, emphatic, and unproblematic features of this problematic play. John and Elinor see and say as much at once when the "good blunt fellow" brashly shows off the qualities that distinguish him so happily from his feeble younger "brother by th' mother's side" in the first scene:

> *Elinor*: He hath a trick of Cordelion's face;
> The accent of his tongue affecteth him.
> Do you not read some tokens of my son

In the large composition of this man?
John: Mine eye hath well examinèd his parts,
And finds them perfect Richard.

(I, i, 163, 71, 85–90)

We are thus assured that we see the very image of the father in the son. Nor is the certainty of his heritage left to the visual proof that surely would suffice in itself. After the Bastard chooses to "take . . . [his] chance" as "the reputed son of Cordelion, / Lord of . . . [his] presence and no land beside" and is dubbed "Sir Richard, and Plantagenet" (136–162), his mother further confirms his birthright: "King Richard Cordelion was thy father" (253). Only the most churlishly rigid moralist in the audience could keep from celebrating this "true" and heroic heritage with Sir Richard or from assenting wholeheartedly to his transformation of his mother's adultery into a sterling virtue:

> Ay, my mother,
> With all my heart I thank thee for my father!
> Who lives and dares but say thou didst not well
> When I was got, I'll send his soul to hell.
> Come, lady, I will show thee to my kin,
> And they shall say, when Richard me begot,
> If thou hadst said him nay, it had been sin.
> Who says it was, he lies; I say 'twas not.

(I, i, 269–276)

Just as clear as the identification of Richard with his father is the sharp contrast between this young embodiment of Cordelion and the "old world" around him. We have already seen this distinction at work, but the association with Cordelion shows even more pointedly in Richard's heroics than in his commentary. It shows most pointedly in his confrontations with Austria through the battlefield scenes in France. However we may come to pity little Arthur and credit his legal claim to the English crown, we can scarcely wish he were wearing that crown or imagine him doing so with sufficient royal "mettle" after we hear him welcome Austria's support in his very first lines:

> God shall forgive you Cordelion's death
> The rather that you give his offspring life,
> Shadowing their right under your wings of war.
> I give you welcome with a powerless hand,
> But with a heart full of unstainèd love.
>
> (II, i, 12–16)

"A heart full of unstained love" is a wonderful thing, and a remarkable one in this play's "iron age," but it is surely not the loutish duke of Austria's due. The Bastard gives Austria his due throughout these sequences in repeated verbal mockery ("And hang a calfskin on those recreant limbs" [III, i, 131, 133]) and, finally, by killing him and retrieving the lionskin that is so patently Sir Richard's rightful heritage. We may suppose that the Bastard wears that emblem thereafter through the play to keep his identification with Cordelion all the more vividly in view for us. In any case, as the "undetermined differences of kings" grows more commodity-stained, the neat hero-versus-poltroon opposition of this personal conflict between Richard and Austria affords a bright contrast to the vexed world of public affairs. We know whom to cheer for here. And though the queasy vileness of John's deadly command to Hubert needs no such gallant heroics to expose it for what it is, its juxtaposition with Richard's triumph over Austria distinguishes the grim reality of the present king all the more sharply from this fictive embodiment of his glorious predecessor. Clearly the Bastard is more "truly" made of royal stuff than John, and it seems only right when he virtually takes over the royal role John is disgracing: "Now hear our English king, / For thus his royalty doth speak in me" (V, ii, 128–129).

But here we enter into matters less clear than the Bastard's identification with Cordelion and his heroic superiority to John and to everyone else in view. To what extent may his embodiment of his royal father be seen in terms of the heroic renewal of the "valiant dead" exemplified by Talbot? Or, contrarily, to what extent does our awareness that the Bastard is a fictive character acting a non-historic role come into play here and modify (or even counter) the idea of actually renewing the heroic past as that idea was represented in the historic figure of Talbot? The fact that the Bastard's role *is* fictive certainly moves us toward the second of these possible ways of understanding it. But since the play itself gives no prominent signals marking off its creative fiction from its historical fact, it is not easy to make confident assertions about our implied awareness of this distinction and its function. It seems reasonable, nonetheless, to say that the more the Bastard impinges on large historical events, the closer he comes to exposing his fictive features openly above the surface. He can bring his personal vendetta against Austria to a conclusion befitting heroic romance without necessarily disrupting our sense that we are watching the "true history" of John's struggle to maintain the crown against Arthur's supporters. But, as already noted, he cannot provide such a happy ending for John's ever-darkening struggle itself. Even by taking command of the English forces in the latter end of that fray, he usurps a role reserved exclusively for historical figures in the other histories and thereby surely stretches to the very limit (if he does not violate) our willingness to credit the represented history as essentially true.[15]

The Bastard does provide the upbeat concluding note to the play with his stirring appeal to England-the-Invincible, but events themselves slip from his grasp and back into their "legitimate" historical course. His own heroics fail when half his forces are "taken by the tide" and "devoured" in the Lincoln washes (V, vi, 39–41), and his brave fictive effort to create a more heroic John ends when he speaks the cruel truth about impending defeat in that anguished monarch's dying ear (V, vii, 49–64). Appropriately, in the "vast confusion" that attends the play's concluding scenes, the truth Richard feels compelled to acknowledge here is false after all. More has taken place than he could know, and the wily Pandulph waits in the wings with a nonheroic compromise solution. The fact that matters are being settled according to the Machiavellian "disposing of the cardinal" may be muted dramatically by keeping him offstage in the finale. That fact nonetheless provides a sinister counterpoint to the ringing theatrical flourish with which the Bastard finally caps things off. Nor can we find much reassurance in Salisbury's prophecy that young Prince Henry, who suddenly appears in the last scene, will "set a form upon that indigest" which his father has "left so shapeless and so rude" (V, vii, 26–27). For one thing, this boy sounds very like the kind but ineffectual Arthur, whom we are not likely to have forgotten so conveniently as the repentant nobles apparently have: "I have a kind soul that would give you thanks, / And knows not how to do it but with tears" (108–109). And for those in the Elizabethan audience who had recently watched the sad story of the Wars of the Roses on this same stage, the newly introduced prince must have sounded (as he does to us) all too much like that other Henry who also came to the throne too young and too weak. Those possessed of the barest historical knowledge would, in any case, immediately perceive the hopes pinned here on Henry III to be false.

I do not mean to make the play and its conclusion too darkly ironic. *King John* does not speak at the end with Pandulph's cynical and chilling voice—which has been overmatched to some extent by events it presumed to control—but with the Bastard's ringing appeal to an image of itself that the English audience is bound to applaud:

> This England never did, nor never shall,
> Lie at the proud foot of a conqueror
> But when it first did help to wound itself.

Now these her princes are come home again,
Come the three corners of the world in arms,
And we shall shock them. Nought shall make us rue
If England to itself do rest but true.

Still, the qualifications lurking in the "if" with which the last line
begins are compounded by the problems (as the play has exposed
them) inherent in the exhortation to be "true." As in the case of
Arthur's death, the truth may not only be hard to swallow; it may
be difficult to determine. And if the Bastard could at that point
remain true to England only by creating a fictive John, we might
also reflect that only this fictive character finds even that "true"
way "among the thorns and dangers" of this play's world.

Certainly the Bastard's fictive status touches (if it does not break)
the surface of this concluding scene, even though he rather reluctantly agrees "to consummate this business happily" according "to
the disposing of the cardinal" rather than taking command of yet
another army he has no historical right to lead (74–96). He
pledges allegiance "with all submission" and "everlastingly" to
young Prince Henry in terms that stress "the *lineal* state and glory
of the land" (101–105). He has been praised by some critics
for doing so and for magnanimously refraining from seizing (or
attempting to seize) the troubled throne himself. Surely that restraint is to his credit, but just as surely this exemplary behavior's
ignoble alternative is impossible within the play's generic terms.
Even to broach the question of such a move on his part is to open
the further question, vital to our understanding of *King John* itself
and of its special place among the histories, of the Bastard's fictive
role in these true events.[16]

As far as the play itself is concerned, if the image of heroic
action that the Bastard both embodies and articulates rings true
(or right) for the English audience, it does so as a fictive ideal to
be emulated and one that stands out in bright contrast with the
true (or actual) course of English history as Shakespeare represents

it here. And this movement of exemplary action into the realm of fiction where it may be distinguished from history is a significant departure from the first tetralogy's initial idea of heroic renewal in history through emulation of the valiant dead. The Bastard is presented, of course, as the "true" (if illegitimate) son and re-embodiment of Cordelion, that exemplary historic hero. But if Cordelion is only recently dead and therefore chronologically not far removed from John's reign, his familiar image nonetheless seems to belong to a lost past, as distant from "this iron age" in which Arthur dies as is Salisbury's fantasy-vision of heroic crusades, and as distinct from "this old world's" actual ways as is the Bastard's fictive presence. If the Bastard is given some fictive grounding in history through his father, at the same time his father's historical precedent seems recoverable in the play's present only by the Bastard's fictive means.

The questions thus posed about the viability of heroic renewal in history also, as they emerge here, disrupt the assumptions about direct continuity between past and present that bolstered the positive example set by Talbot and took a sterner form in the retributive scheme of *Richard III*. No assurance about providential justice comforts us as we watch John stumble into evil in a world where the Church's legate mocks belief in signs from heaven (III, iv, 153–159). And the best of the past seems not only remote but distinct in kind from the actual and deplorable present, whether that better image is seen in the historically remembered Cordelion or in his fictively imagined son. If *King John* remains a problem play for many readers, it surely shows its own awareness of such problems as these in its representation of both the truths and the "fictions of history."[17] In doing so, it anticipates the second tetralogy, where the difficulty of knowing and recovering historical truth, the disparity between the evoked heroic past and the present's harsh experience, and the relationship of creative fiction to true history continue to be central concerns.

CHAPTER FIVE

Richard II

"Let Not Tomorrow Then Ensue Today"

Like the three parts of *Henry VI*, *Richard II* dramatizes the forcible replacement of an ineffectual king, son to a heroic father, by an apparently more able leader and ends by emphasizing the unstable condition of the new ruler's regime. In both cases, for those who do remember, the son's shortcomings are all the more sharply outlined by the recollected light of the father's virtues. But, as we have seen, the progressively deteriorating situation through the earlier trilogy is marked by growing "neglection" of the heroic past. And in *Richard II*, as the "skipping king" gives way to "grim necessity" in the person of Bolingbroke, their heroic predecessors and the past in which they flourished seem even more radically lost. It is not just that things are getting worse as sons fail to

emulate exemplary fathers or harden their fathers' dangerous will-
fulness into willed villainy, which was the sorry case in the second
and third parts of *Henry VI*. It is as though the succession that
linked son to father is broken altogether; as though the glorious
past not only fades and is forgotten but has no functional relationship with "this new world" in which former heroic models
would seem alien and out of place. At the end the new king, already "full of woe," looks far away to the Holy Land in what we
know to be a futile hope for a redemptive crusade. Neither he nor
anyone else, however, any longer looks back to the valiant dead
who preceded him or attempts to redeem the present time by
awakening the spirit of the past.

Those valiant dead, "the Black Prince, that young Mars of men"
(II, iii, 101) and his father, Edward III, are prominently recalled
through the first half of the play. But it is significant that they are
remembered almost exclusively by the aged survivors of the Black
Prince's own generation—by his brothers, "old John of Gaunt,
time-honored Lancaster" (I, i, 1) and the duke of York, "now
prisoner to the palsy" (II, iii, 104), and by the widowed duchess
of Gloucester. Insofar as the departed heroes "live" at all, they live
in memories that are now expiring, not as models who are revived
by a new generation. And the roles these few survivors play, as
well as the nature of their recollections, enforce the sense that the
past they remember (and still in some measure attempt to represent) is being lost, that it serves no vital function for a present in
which they themselves feel lost at best.

Again, comparison with *1 Henry VI*, in which the situation is
in many ways so similar, suggests the different sense we get of the
change taking place in *Richard II*. In the earlier play the duke of
Bedford, surviving brother to the dead hero, despite his funeral-
procession lament that "arms avail not, now that Henry's dead,"
still carries his brother's heroic spirit into the bereaved and worsening present. When he dies, he does so, despite age and illness,
in a way that consciously lives up to his heroic heritage as he

understands it from history. Brought before the walls of Rouen "sick in a chair," he refuses to be carried from the scene of battle to "some better place":

> For once I read
> That stout Pendragon in his litter sick
> Came to the field and vanquishèd his foes.
> Methinks I should revive the soldiers' hearts,
> Because I ever found them as myself.
>
> (III, ii, 94–98)

And his onstage auditors accord him the tribute such a valiant final gesture deserves:

> Undaunted spirit in a dying breast!
>
> .   .   .   .
>
> Let's not forget
> The noble Duke of Bedford, late deceased,
> But see his exequies fulfilled in Roan.
> A braver soldier never couchèd lance,
> A gentler heart did never sway in court.
>
> (99–135)

"Let's not forget"! As we noted earlier, it is, appropriately, Talbot who speaks here, and his words insist on the continuity that should keep the "undaunted spirit" embodied by Bedford alive from age to age.

By contrast, the dying Gaunt's final scene features his famous set piece in which the model portrait of England is held up only to be shattered by the "shameful conquest" the debased England of the present has made of its true self. Like the queen who later terms Richard's undoing "a second fall of cursèd man" (III, iv, 76), Gaunt's description of the England-that-was as "this other Eden, demi-paradise," suggests a fundamental loss, a basic change in the condition of things, not just a worsening situation.[1] It is true that Gaunt, buoying himself for the purpose with a host of formulaic old saws, intends (despite York's discouragement) to breathe his last "in wholesome counsel to . . . [Richard's] unstaid youth" and therefore at least persuades himself to hope that reform—the restoration of things as they were and should be—is still possible. And it is true that his inspired expiring vision of "this scept'red isle" in its "proper" image seems cast, as he develops it for eighteen lines, in a virtually eternal present rather than being thrust retrospectively into the past. Could such a "fortress built by Nature," such a "happy breed of men," ever fall or falter? The verbs and participles all suggest a continuous present, and therefore even those "royal kings" whose "renownèd . . . deeds" and chivalric crusades must necessarily belong to English history if Gaunt were to give them names (Edward III? Richard I?) are invoked not as past heroes but as timeless beings created out of England's continuously "teeming womb" (II, i, 40–56). But when the anguished turn finally comes, when "this dear dear land / . . . *Is now* leased out . . . / Like to a tenement or pelting farm" (57–60; emphasis added), the transformation from the posited model to the present cruel reality seems so extreme as to be an irreversible change in kind, not a temporary decline. The felt difference between king and landlord, between sceptered isle and tenement is not merely one of degree, as Gaunt expresses it. And he finally does relegate to the past the England that had seemed so permanently ordained by Nature: "That England that *was wont* to conquer others / Hath made a shameful conquest of itself" (65–66; emphasis added).

We need not suppose that Gaunt, for all his deathbed sense of himself as a "prophet new-inspired," clearly foresees an ever-fallen future or fully gives up to an irretrievable past his idea of England as "this earth of majesty." The latter vision is too compelling for him, and though he knows that the current scandal will not vanish with his expiring life (67), it would be overstating the point here to suggest that he consciously dooms his "blessed plot" to per-petual bondage as a pelting farm. But *our* perspective on Gaunt's image of England as it "was wont" to be includes the fact that he, the guardian of that vision, is dying and that there is no young successor to renew or sustain it in "this new world." Richard, for whose ears Gaunt is presumably saving his remaining breath, does not even hear this grand epitaph to the sceptered isle he is now leasing out so shamefully. The prophet spends himself on this vision before the careless king and his entourage arrive. We will return to the significance of the actual final exchange between the dying uncle and his royal nephew in a moment.[2]

Those other voices of memory, the duchess of Gloucester and the duke of York, give us the same sense that the heroic past is lost—indeed, that it is being violently rooted out—in the present. The duchess's plea that Gaunt should avenge his brother, her murdered husband, begins with this elegy for the faded sons of noble Edward:

> Hath love in thy old blood no living fire?
> Edward's seven sons, whereof thyself art one,
> Were as seven vials of his sacred blood,
> Or seven fair branches springing from one root.
> Some of those seven are dried by nature's course,
> Some of those branches by the Destinies cut;
> But Thomas, my dear lord, my life, my Gloucester,
> One vial full of Edward's sacred blood,
> One flourishing branch of his most royal root,
> Is cracked, and all the precious liquor spilt,
> Is hacked down, and his summer leaves all faded,
> By envy's hand and murder's bloody axe.
>
> (I, ii, 10–21)

Whatever "living fire" survives in her "old blood" expires, like Gaunt's, early in the play. The report of her death in II, ii merely gives official confirmation to her own clear assertion that her leavetaking in this second scene, as she returns to the "empty lodgings and unfurnished walls, / Unpeopled offices, untrodden stones" of her widowed Plashy, is a final one, both to Gaunt and to the world that has destroyed and forsaken her:

Farewell, old Gaunt. Thy sometimes brother's wife
With her companion, Grief, must end her life.

.   .   .   .

Desolate, desolate will I hence and die!
The last leave of thee takes my weeping eye.

(54–74)

Even her memory of noble Edward and his seven sons focuses on
the dried branches and faded leaves of those she recalls. And with
her early passing, as with Gaunt's, we see such memories themselves fading away.

Unlike his brother and his sister-in-law, York survives his nephew
Richard and accommodates himself to the "new world" of his
other nephew, Bolingbroke. York recalls the lost heritage of his
generation more fully than do these other two, and the nature of
his survival and accommodation tells us even more about the rupture with the past than do their deaths. As with Gaunt, comparison with York's counterpart in the *Henry VI* plays helps to clarify
the sense of just what has been lost here. Like York, who lives
on as "the last of noble Edward's sons" after Gaunt's death,
Humphrey, duke of Gloucester survives his brother Bedford and,
again like York, both recalls the past and attempts to maintain its
virtues in a present that dismays him. Indeed, Gloucester's dismay
at the foreseen effect of Henry's foolish marriage to the dowerless
Margaret is expressed in terms that might largely apply to the loss
of the past in the present that York deplores in *Richard II*:

O peers of England, shameful is this league.
Fatal this marriage, cancelling your fame,
Blotting your names from books of memory.
Rasing the characters of your renown,
Defacing monuments of conquered France,
Undoing all as all had never been!

(2*HVI* I, i, 96–101)

Blotting memory, erasing renown, defacing monuments—these
are, as we have seen, the awful opposites of the proper emulation

that awakens remembrance of the valiant dead and renews their deeds. And when Gloucester sums up this negation as "undoing all as all had never been," he might well speak for York as that harried elder likewise recalls his heroic brother's deeds and laments their undoing by his nephew's inglorious hand:

> I am the last of noble Edward's sons,
> Of whom thy father, Prince of Wales, was first.
> In war was never lion raged more fierce,
> In peace was never gentle lamb more mild,
> Than was that young and princely gentleman.
> His face thou hast, for even so looked he,
> Accomplished with the number of thy hours;
> But when he frowned, it was against the French
> And not against his friends. His noble hand
> Did win what he did spend, and spent not that
> Which his triumphant father's hand had won.
> His hands were guilty of no kinred blood,
> But bloody with the enemies of his kin.
>   (II, i, 171–183)

But if York's grievance includes Gloucester's dismay that the son spends what the father gained, he sees another dimension in the "undoing" that confronts him. For Gloucester, "undoing" was precisely the loss of lands won, the negation of accomplishment which amounts (rather more figuratively than literally) to erasure of the accomplisher's renown. And despite Warwick's responsive tears because the extent and strategic location of the lost territories put them practically "past recovery" for his sword, nothing has so altered his and Gloucester's world that what has been carelessly thrown away could never conceivably be recovered. But as York points out with such anguish, Richard's obliteration of Hereford's right to inherit the Lancastrian property (not just his seizure of the property itself) sunders the very process of succession that gives the present (including Richard himself) its identity, its being, in terms of the past:

> Take Hereford's rights away, and take from Time
> His charters and his customary rights;
> Let not to-morrow then ensue to-day;
> Be not thyself—for how art thou a king
> But by fair sequence and succession?
>
> (195–199)

The order that the horrified York sees being broken here is not just a static Chain of Being or Degree but the temporal continuity that defines the present structure by inheritance from the past. And with "sequence and succession" thus shattered, the present he sees suffers more than a loss of memory or of lands. It loses "itself," its means of determining who is king or subject, what is right or wrong (or the only means of doing so that York knows and credits), and he therefore feels helplessly lost in it:

> God for his mercy! What a tide of woes
> Comes rushing on this woeful land at once!
> I know not what to do.
>
> (II, ii, 98–100)

Confronting in the person of his other nephew the rising tide of power politics that Richard's heedless action has unloosed, York can only yearn wistfully for the time when his might could enforce what he saw to be right:

> Were I but now lord of such hot youth
> As when brave Gaunt thy father and myself
> Rescued the Black Prince, that young Mars of men,
> From forth the ranks of many thousand French,
> O, then how quickly should this arm of mine,
> Now prisoner to the palsy, chastise thee
> And minister correction to thy fault!
>
> (II, iii, 99–105)

"O, then . . . !" But the vigorous action of that lost time and its lost leader, the Black Prince, are as alien to the present time as the palsied arm of York is incapable of setting it right. By the fading light of his past, York still believes that might does not make right ("to find out right with wrong—it may not be" [145]). But seeing only wrongs and no right around him and confessing that his "power is weak and all ill left," this last relic of a vanished era first pronounces himself a "neuter" and then only pauses on the brink of breaking his "country's laws" as he has always known them before falling in with his inexorably advancing nephew: "Things past redress are now with me past care" (152–171). Again, the contrast with Gloucester, though it obviously reflects character as well as situation, is instructive. When he eschews his fallen wife's warning against the snares of his enemies, Gloucester may be naively overconfident that others will act, as he does, in accordance with the law:

> I must offend before I be attainted;
> And had I twenty times so many foes,
> And each of them had twenty times their power,
> All these could not procure me any scathe
> So long as I am loyal, true, and crimeless.
>
> (*2HVI*, II, iv, 59–63)

But if others break the laws to bring him down, the steady firmness with which he adheres to justice and with which he meets his undoing when it comes is threatened by no realization that the foundation of law itself is lost. The latter is York's case, and in a world bereft of Time's charters themselves (and thus "past redress") he drifts despite his reluctance into Bolingbroke's rapidly expanding camp. Once there, he attempts, as we shall see, to construct a new basis for succession and hence for right action. But this "last of noble Edward's sons" never again looks back to take his bearings by noble Edward's time or recalls "the Black Prince, that young Mars of men." For him, as for everyone else, that heroic past is now lost indeed.

That these elders are the primary spokesmen in the play for history so recent that it highlights their own youth, and that they dwell on invidious comparisons between their heyday and what they perceive to be a scandalous present, is scarcely surprising, however significant it may be for our view of the change under way.[3] What is more surprising and certainly more instrumental in that change is the nature of Richard's responses to their recollections and his very different attitude toward the past. To a certain extent, this difference fits stereotypical expectations about generational conflicts over old ways and new on his side as well as theirs. Before he is shocked into articulating the profound implications of Richard's appropriation of his cousin's inheritance, York, as prone to conventional phrasing as his brother, expresses his skepticism about the effect of "wholesome counsel" on Richard's "ear of youth" in just such stereotypical terms:

> No; it is stopped with other, flattering sounds,
> As praises, of whose taste the wise are fond,
> Lascivious metres, to whose venom sound
> The open ear of youth doth always listen;
> Report of fashions in proud Italy,
> Whose manners still our tardy apish nation
> Limps after in base imitation.
> Where doth the world thrust forth a vanity
> (So be it new, there's no respect how vile)
> That is not quickly buzzed into his ears?
> Then all too late comes counsel to be heard
> Where will doth mutiny with wit's regard.[4]
>
> (II, i, 17–28)

Any individualizing traits disappear in the formulaic youth who "doth always listen" to the enticing call of newfangledness (with the customary taint of "proud Italy" on it) and to the flatterers who sweeten their "venom" with praise. But nothing in the dialogue actually given to Richard or to that hapless trio dubbed "caterpillars" by his enemies fills out (or even necessarily fits) this stencilled portrait (though producers may choose to follow its pattern for costuming and staging). And in fact, Richard's most significant features extend beyond the stereotype.

Carelessness, of course, *is* a common feature of wayward youth, and the young king's flagrant carelessness certainly impresses his observers onstage and off—nowhere more so than in the sequence immediately following Gaunt's death. The flippancy of his momentary adaptation of Gaunt's own hackneyed proverbial mode as a response to the solemn occasion ("The ripest fruit first falls, and so doth he; / His time is spent, our pilgrimage must be") is underscored by his abrupt dismissal of the subject altogether: "So much for that!" (II, i, 153–155). And his obliviousness to the gist of York's outbursts when he promptly confiscates Gaunt's (now Hereford's) property ("Why, uncle, what's the matter?") is underscored even more pointedly when Richard names the disaffected old man (whose "tender patience" he has just pricked "to those thoughts / Which honor and allegiance cannot think") lord governor of England during his pending absence in Ireland because York "is just and always loved us well" (186–221). Of special significance, however, is one dimension of Richard's carelessness, prominent in this sequence and consistent throughout—and that is his utter disregard for the past in general and his own heritage in particular.

Here we find a facet of the young king that seems surprising enough to border on paradox. One delusive prop of his carelessness, of course, is his faulty (and by mid-play faltering) assumption that his royal blood is somehow inviolable and invulnerable:

> Not all the water in the rough rude sea
> Can wash the balm off from an anointed king.
> The breath of worldly men cannot depose
> The deputy elected by the Lord.
>
> (III, ii, 54–57)

But though he makes so much of his "sacred blood," it is as though, for him, it has no source, as though it were simply a given

of his condition, a unique endowment of the "anointed king . . .
elected by the Lord." When the duchess of Gloucester twice echoes
the term that Richard first uses in the opening scene (119), it is
with quite natural reference to the line (the root and its branches)
through which such royal blood flows, so that the seven sons
are as "vials" preserving their father Edward's "sacred blood"
(I, ii, 12, 17). It is never so for Richard, whose royalty acknowledges no root.

This "neglection" is all the more remarkable in Richard as the
son and grandson of those far-famed heroes who are otherwise so
often remembered through the first part of the play—that is,
through his own tenure as king in the play. His total unresponsive-
ness to (and evident incomprehension of) York's anguished evocation of the Black Prince's noble image is perfectly characteristic in
this respect. In similar circumstances, we heard Henry VI express
his full (and understandable) consciousness both of his heroic
father and of his own deviation from his heritage, defending the
latter with an apparent mixture of saintliness and petulance:

> I'll leave my son my virtuous deeds behind,
> And would my father had left me no more.
> For all the rest is held at such a rate
> As brings a thousandfold more care to keep
> Than in possession any jot of pleasure.
>
> (*3HVI*, II, ii, 49–53)

But unlike Gaunt's charge that Richard should have been deposed before he was ever crowned and that he is now effectually
deposing himself, York's account of the radical difference between
father and son (so barbed, with its explicit reference to the murder
of Gloucester, that York virtually apologizes for his *lèse majesté*)
stirs, as we have seen, nothing more than unconcern and evident
puzzlement in the young king (II, i, 184–188). Rather than
touching a nerve, York is addressing a blank spot in Richard's
makeup. In a play that is filled (up to the deposition) with remi-

niscences, Richard never looks back to the past and only once alludes even obliquely to his unique heroic heritage (who else among Shakespeare's kings could boast of both a father and a grandfather of such mythic stature?).[5]

This is the passive side of Richard's curiously "unhistorical" stance—his total neglect of those valiant dead who should lend such luster to his precious royal blood. The active side, manifest both in attitude and action, amounts to the virtual opposite (not just negligence) of heroic renewal that restores life to (and gains vitality from) remembered precursors. Instead of awakening remembrance by emulating their deeds, Richard, like death itself, destroys and buries his "fathers" and forefathers, "undoing all as all had never been." The fullest display of this inversion comes in Gaunt's final scene. Both coolly (before he arrives [I, iv, 59–64]) and heatedly (after Gaunt delivers his "wholesome counsel" more in anger than in sorrow), the young king wishes his old uncle dead. And their exchange illustrates Richard's odd conception of his "royal blood," which detaches him (and it) from any familial or historical connection, as well as his willingness to shed the blood that would be "his" if he acknowledged such connections. In this respect he is, if less self-consciously and therefore less villainously, "himself alone," like that other Richard.

Gaunt alters their scene from banter ("Can sick men play so nicely with their names?") to a serious thing by reversing their roles and naming Richard the deathly ill patient, careless of his condition. Then, characteristically looking back more than ahead, the dying "prophet" wishfully reconstructs a history that might have been if "noble Edward" had been a prophet indeed:

> O, had thy grandsire, with a prophet's eye,
> Seen how his son's son, should destroy his sons,
> From forth thy reach he would have laid thy shame,
> Deposing thee before thou wert possessed,
> Which art possessed now to depose thyself.

> (II, i, 104–108)

This heated (surely not "frozen," as Richard terms it) admonition, by contrast with York's, which follows hard upon, stings Richard's "royal blood" to "fury"—not, evidently, because it sets him against his father's heritage (York's will do that just as emphatically) but because it dwells on deposition and verbally strips Richard of his "right royal majesty": "Landlord of England art thou now, not king" (113). Richard's fiery and insistently "regal" response includes the single reference he makes to his father in the entire play:

> Darest [thou] with thy frozen admonition
> Make pale our cheek, chasing the royal blood
> With fury from his native residence.
> Now, by my seat's right royal majesty,
> Wert thou not brother to great Edward's son,
> This tongue that runs so roundly in thy head
> Should run thy head from thy unreverent shoulders.
>
> (117–123)

But note that even here Richard mutes the implicit connection between the royal blood that has its "native residence" in his countenance and his descent from "great Edward's son." It is primarily as Gaunt's brother rather than his own father that the Black Prince gains whatever sway he has in Richard's conscience here.

Gaunt's reply, rather than simply remarking on the impotent absurdity of threatening a dying man with execution, spells out the full implications of Richard's stance toward his heritage:

> O, spare me not, my brother Edward's son,
> For that I was his father Edward's son!
> That blood already, like the pelican,
> Hast thou tapped out and drunkenly caroused.
> My brother Gloucester, plain well-meaning soul—
> Whom fair befall in heaven 'mongst happy souls!—
> May be a precedent and witness good
> That thou respect'st not spilling Edward's blood.

Join with the present sickness that I have,
And thy unkindness be like crooked age,
To crop at once a too-long-withered flower.

$$(124-134)$$

Gaunt insists on the connection that Richard had grudgingly acknowledged here and elsewhere ignores altogether—on the confluence of the blood that runs from father to son and brother to brother. And by identifying Richard as the young pelican who drinks his *parent's* blood, Gaunt reinforces the duchess of Gloucester's argument that spilling a "vial" of Edward's blood (or accepting a brother's death without retaliation) is equivalent to both patricide and suicide:

Ah, Gaunt, his blood was thine! That bed, that womb,
That metal, that self mould that fashioned thee,
Made him a man; and though thou livest and breathest,
Yet art thou slain in him. Thou dost consent
In some large measure to thy father's death
In that thou seest thy wretched brother die,
Who was the model of thy father's life.

(I, ii, 22–28)

Just so, in Gaunt's figurative terms, by killing one uncle and willing another's death, Richard has "tapped out" his own father's blood. Rather than renewing the Black Prince through youthful emulation as a proper "model of . . . [his] father's life," Richard, as Gaunt makes clear, unnaturally behaves "like crooked age" and joins with sickness to crop the "too-long withered flower" that carries the same blood and is of the "self mould" as his father.[6]

If Richard thus inverts the ideal of renewing his heroic father (or "fathers") through active remembrance in the present, that ideal finds its spokesman early in the play in the person of Bolingbroke, Richard's opposite in so many ways. "Lusty, young, and cheerly drawing breath" as he enters the lists against Mowbray, Bolingbroke addresses his father in terms that insist both on the

paternal source of his blood and on his commitment to revive old
Gaunt in his own "lusty havior":

> O thou, the earthly author of my blood,
> Whose youthful spirit, in me regenerate,
> Doth with a twofold vigor lift me up
> To reach at victory above my head,
> Add proof unto mine armor with thy prayers,
> And with thy blessings steel my lance's point,
> That it may enter Mowbray's waxen coat
> And furbish new the name of John a Gaunt
> Even in the lusty havior of his son.
>
> (I, iii, 69–77)

The father inspires the son and the son revives the father. In keeping with the "twofold vigor" of this spirit, which serves as an
evidently positive counterpart to Richard's negligence of his heritage, all early references Bolingbroke makes to his "high blood's
royalty" are placed in the proper context of "the glorious worth
of . . . [his] descent" (I, i, 71, 107). But all such reference (and
deference) to his lineage ceases when he assumes royal power in
what can only be his "own" right. When it serves his purpose as
he moves toward the throne, he uses the language of Gaunt and
the duchess of Gloucester that identifies son with father and
brother with brother. He speaks thus as he "becomes" Lancaster
and confronts the still resistant York:

> As I was banished, I was banished Hereford;
> But as I come, I come for Lancaster.
> And, noble uncle, I beseech your grace
> Look on my wrongs with an indifferent eye.
> You are my father, for methinks in you
> I see old Gaunt alive. O, then, my father,
> Will you permit that I shall stand condemned . . . ?

.   .   .   .

I lay my claim
To my inheritance of free descent.
                    (II, iii, 113–136)

The terms may be "right" so far as they go, but they are also
self-serving enough to seem sophistical, glossing over as they do
the hard fact that Bolingbroke does not so much "lay his claim"
as force it "in braving arms" (143). York, before he capitulates
to "things past redress," cuts through his nephew's case clearly
enough with his simple, single-edged maxim: "To find out right
with wrong—it may not be" (171, 145). Shortly thereafter,
on the very brink of usurpation, Bolingbroke salutes Richard
(through Northumberland's embassy) with the sort of reference
to their heritage that Richard himself never makes, though here,
despite his posited humble posture, the virtual equivalence suggested in their "royalties" stemming from the same "royal grandsire" may tell us more about the opaque usurper's designs than he
himself ever does:

Thy thrice-noble cousin
Harry Bolingbroke doth humbly kiss thy hand;
And by the honorable tomb he swears
That stands upon your royal grandsire's bones,
And by the royalties of both your bloods
(Currents that spring from one most gracious head),
And by the buried hand of warlike Gaunt,
And by the worth and honor of himself,
Comprising all that may be sworn or said,
His coming hither hath no further scope
Than for his lineal royalties, and to beg
Enfranchisement immediate on his knees.
                    (III, iii, 103–114)

But once Richard's "linear royalty" has actually been violated
(along with this profuse oath disclaiming that purpose), all such

terms disappear from the lines of the new king and his party—
and indeed from the play itself.

It would not suit the promoters of Bolingbroke's "new world,"
of course, to awake remembrance of a heritage that could only
highlight their unwarranted seizure of the crown. Northumberland and his eager recruits had first faulted the "most degenerate"
King Richard in terms used by Henry VI's partisan Lancastrian
critics (Gloucester, Clifford) as well as by his Yorkist foes:

> For warred he hath not,
> But basely yielded upon compromise
> That which his noble ancestors achieved with blows.

And they then spoke (in no very specific way, to be sure) of
renewal and restoration rather than rebellion:

> We shall shake off our slavish yoke,
> Imp out our drooping country's broken wing,
> Redeem from broking pawn the blemished crown,
> Wipe off the dust that hides our sceptre's gilt,
> And make high majesty look like itself.
>
> (II, i, 252–295)

How much Northumberland actually foresees at this point of the
new world he is helping to usher in is as much a matter of speculation as the "silent king's" original aims. But in any case, once
he is installed, neither Bolingbroke nor his foremost henchman
shows any more recollection of high majesty's "noble ancestors"
than Richard ever had.

The only attempt made to legitimize the new regime comes in
a form that virtually parodies the equivalence of uncle with father
and brother with brother by confluence of "blood" that had been
an article of faith for the older generation and at least a matter
of lip service for the younger Bolingbroke. Richard had relin-
quished himself to Bolingbroke's compelling force with a characteristically sardonic observation on their relationship: "Cousin, I

am too young to be your father, / Though you are old enough to be my heir" (III, iii, 204–205). When the transfer of the crown is publicly staged, official credence is given to the absurdity that Richard's bitter quip had mocked. Perhaps York, the last vestige of noble ancestry, persuades himself that Time's charters can be restored by construing Richard as his cousin's father. In any case, it is York who offers the formal pronouncement to that effect, thereby converting the duke of Lancaster into Henry IV:

> Great Duke of Lancaster, I come to thee
> From plume-plucked Richard, who with willing soul
> Adopts thee heir and his high sceptre yields
> To the possession of thy royal hand.
> Ascend his throne, descending now from him,
> And long live Henry, fourth of that name!
>
> (IV, i, 107–112)

The "glorious worth" of Bolingbroke's once much-touted descent (I, i, 107) is thus transmuted, so that in ascending the throne he now descends from Richard alone, and their true fathers and majestic grandfather are never mentioned again.

The strain of stifling the past he remembered so nostalgically and thus redefining Time's "charters and his customary rights" surely shows in York's desperate fealty to "the new-made king" he has finally helped to "ascend" (V, ii, 45–47). Again, comparison with York's prototype in the *Henry VI* series may suggest the more radically unsettling nature of the "fearful change" under way in *Richard II*. Like York, Gloucester had placed loyalty to the state above family ties when he acquiesced in his wife's arrest and conviction for the treasonous dealings to which her "aspiring humor" had prompted her. But, for all his grief, the quiet firmness with which Gloucester meets this ordeal bespeaks the simple clarity of the case as he sees it in terms of the established laws he honors and upholds: "Eleanor, the law, thou seest, hath judgèd thee. / I cannot justify whom the law condemns" (*2HVI*, II, iii, 15–16).

By contrast, the frenzy with which York turns on his son Aumerle for supporting the former king against his "heir" suggests the tension underlying the old man's adaptation to "the green lap of this new-come spring." He has just schooled his duchess in the redefining and renaming that "this new spring of time" requires:

> *Duchess*: Here comes my son Aumerle.
> *York*: Aumerle that was;
> But that is lost for being Richard's friend,
> And, madam, you must call him Rutland now.
> (V, ii, 41–43)

Essential mother that she is, the duchess simply ignores such official transformations and addresses the young man by the only title that really matters to her: "Welcome, my son" (46). But when York shows Henry the document that proves his renamed son's "treason," Rutland demonstrates his capacity to "bear himself well" in a world that thus reconstitutes itself by unwriting (or effectively erasing and ignoring) its past:

> Remember, as thou read'st, thy promise passed.
> *I do repent me. Read not my name there.*
> My heart is not confederate with my hand.
> (V, iii, 51–53; emphasis added)

And York shows the fury of his own conversion by arguing for Rutland's execution in terms that reverse the "old" (and now evidently forgotten) idea, once espoused so vibrantly by Bolingbroke, that the father is regenerated "even in the lusty havior of his son":

> Mine honor lives when his dishonor dies,
> Or my shamed life in his dishonor lies.
> Thou kill'st me in his life; giving him breath,
> The traitor lives, the true man's put to death.
> (70–73)

"Thou kill'st me in . . . [thy] life." York's eldest brother might bring that same charge against *his* son Richard, who by sheer neglect fails to renew his father's glory in his own life and fails (as York had lamented) even to retain what the Black Prince had won. And Richard's "fathers" by extension, Gaunt and Glouces-ter, could make the charge more directly—even literally, in the latter's case. As we have seen, both the active and passive aspects of Richard's patricidal attitude toward his heritage are empha-sized in his earlier, careless phase when, as king, he more than anyone else should have sustained the vitality of England's "royal blood." With the loss of his all-too-hollow crown comes the growth in awareness of his own mortality and humanity that makes this play as much *The Tragedy of Richard the Second* as it is the "history" of one reign's sorry end and another's troubled beginning. For all his growth in self-awareness, however, Richard gains through his suffering absolutely nothing in the way of historical consciousness or interest in the past. He may be able to predict accurately enough, on the basis of his own experience with them, the future strife between Northumberland and Henry (V, i, 55–68), but he never looks back beyond (or behind) his own experience. Where memory is concerned, even as a source of the suffering that brings what wisdom he attains, his focus re-mains limited entirely to himself:

> Or that I could forget what I have been!
> Or not remember what I must be now!
>
> (III, iii, 138–139)

> Yet I well remember
> The favors of these men. Were they not mine?
> Did they not sometime cry "All hail!" to me?
> So Judas did to Christ; but he, in twelve,
> Found truth in all but one; I, in twelve thousand none.
>
> (IV, i, 167–171)

> Learn, good soul,
> To think our former state a happy dream;
> From which awaked, the truth of what we are
> Shows us but this. I am sworn brother, sweet,
> To grim Necessity, and he and I
> Will keep a league till death.
>
> (V, i, 17–22)

In this limited retrospect, which ignores the longer and broader historical past entirely, Richard remains at one both with his earlier self and (in this regard alone) with the new regime, which has no stake in remembering anything that preceded Richard, the "father" from whom it claims "descent." The deposed king's consuming interest is in the "book" that is himself, though his aversion to what is "upon record" extends, not unnaturally, to the written account of his own folly which, for all his reluctant willingness to "undo" himself publicly, Richard refuses "to read a public lecture of" (IV, i, 203–232, 273–275). Even when his final reflection focuses specifically on the subject of time, the brief and generalized summation of his past and present ("I wasted time, and now doth time waste me") turns quickly into a philosophical conceit likening Richard to a clock and away from any examination of the backward abyss which remains for him more blank than dark (V, v, 41–66).

It is appropriate, therefore, not only to his "tragic" conception of his experience but to his unhistorical sense of himself that Richard so readily chooses the *de casibus* mode for his "story," both at the first wave of adversity, when he would "sit upon the ground / And tell sad stories of the death of kings" (III, ii, 155 ff.), and at the last parting from his tristful queen, whom he bids eke out her exile by telling "the lamentable tale of me" (V, i, 40–50). *De casibus* tragedy, with its "tales / Of woeful ages long ago betid," is Richard's closest approximation to looking back in time. But with its perfectly repetitive pattern, it is perfectly unhistorical in essence, since time brings no meaningful succession of persons or events, acting only as the constant agent of dusty death and destroying every king alike regardless of his accomplishments. *De casibus* tragedy shares only its emphasis on recurrence with heroical history. Otherwise, the two modes are antithetical, with one featuring the single and inexorable force of Death, who scoffs at state and grins at pomp, while the other celebrates the immortal fame that lives "despite of death" (I, i, 168) and is renewed (repetition's positive aspect) through emulation that "awake[s] remembrance of these valiant dead." It is fitting that Richard, who ignores and thwarts remembrance of his heroic heritage and has to be chidingly reminded by the bishop of Carlisle that to "fight and die is death destroying death" (III, ii, 184), should give his story over thus to Death's own monotonous genre.

If both winners and losers, for differing reasons, let sleeping neglection blot out England's proud history, none can escape the actual consequences of the past or silence all retrospect. With its inspirational and vitalizing potential stifled, recollection of recent history asserts itself in the destructive form that sows discord through this play and its two sequels bearing Henry's title. The very scene in which Henry publicly "accepts" the crown begins with a nasty reprise of the opening quarrel between Mowbray and Bolingbroke, based as it was on contradictory versions of past deeds and centering on the death of Gloucester. But whereas the mutual and comprehensive accusations of the earlier dispute ("*all* the treasons for these eighteen years / Complotted and contrivèd in this land / Fetch from false Mowbray their first head and spring" [I, i, 95–97; emphasis added]) were shrouded in vague allusions (probably because of Richard's presence), the crescendo of charges and countercharges that mars King Henry's debut is laden with the sort of reportorial detail by ear- and eyewitnesses that should compel ready belief:

> I heard you say, "Is not my arm of length,
> That reacheth from the restful English court

As far as Calais to mine uncle's head?"
Amongst much other talk that very time
I heard you say that you had rather refuse
The offer of an hundred thousand crowns
Than Bolingbroke's return to England;
Adding withal, how blest this land would be
In this your cousin's death.

(IV, i, 11–19)

Such a vivid account seems to open a window onto "that very time," so that we gain direct access to the otherwise darkened past. But Bagot's glib memory virtually refutes itself, stumbling over the specific details with which it should be piling up credit. The "time when Gloucester's death was plotted" simply cannot be "that very time" when Aumerle allegedly opposed Bolingbroke's return from banishment since, as even an otherwise uninformed audience knows from the play itself, the former "time" preceded the latter by a quite considerable gap. And, as the gauges begin to fly, those precise reporters who do not contradict themselves flatly contradict one another:

> *Surrey*: My Lord Fitzwater, I do remember well
> The very time Aumerle and you did talk.
> *Fitzwater*: 'Tis very true. You were in presence then,
> And you can witness with me this is true.
> *Surrey*: As false, by heaven, as heaven itself is true!

(60–64)

Whatever *was* history's truth is hopelessly mangled in competing recollections of it. If the object of heroical history is to invigorate the present by awakening remembrance of the past and thus to make the best of the past live anew in the present, here we see a use of the past that has precisely the opposite effect. Whatever his own meager imagination intends when he coins the phrase, Bagot appropriately introduces this whole series of reconstructions by referring his auditors back to "that dead time"—dead insofar as its true life can never be revived through such a maze of self-serving revisions, and dead insofar as it haunts the present like a destructive ghost in the varying shapes these wranglers give it, rather than inspiring the present to emulate its vital image. Nor are such mundane ghosts in the service of a sure and "true" providential justice, as were those who announced the high All-seer's impending doom in *Richard III* just before all wrongs were finally righted. Rather, these visions and revisions continue to confound the factions of "this new world" throughout Henry's troublesome reign as Shakespeare will dramatize it. Put to uncreative purposes by uncreative minds, such faulty (and in every sense partial) recollections scarcely deserve to be called "fictions of history." Only Henry's "unthrifty son" and his less thrifty foil will use memory imaginatively enough to transform it into the "true" realm of fiction.

The strong positives and negatives emphasized in this account of *Richard II* may seem to suggest a simple moral reading of the loss that it dramatizes ("Don't forget your father or the Bolingbroke will get you!"). Surely Richard's "waste" of past time and the consequent eclipse of the noble heritage that might inspire the present is seen negatively, but scarcely in such complacently didactic terms. One complicating factor is the actual (or "historical") status of that noble heritage itself as the play presents it to us. We are given no reason to doubt the well-chronicled heroics of the Black Prince or to question the magnificence of his "mountain sire." But we are given every reason to suppose that the image of their era has been improved in the aged memories that invoke it here. Both Gaunt and York, as we have seen, are fond of easily phrased proverbs and clichés.[7] York's description of the Black Prince thus falls into prefabricated patterns that can scarcely accommodate the whole truth ("In war was never lion raged more fierce, / In peace was never gentle lamb more mild" [II, i, 173–174]).[8] Any view of a better past that is converted through Richard's negligence and Bolingbroke's opportunism into a worse present ought to take into account the possible degree to which the play shows us a happily idealized past that is increasingly ignored by an unpleasantly "real" present.

But this question of a fictive ideal juxtaposed with problematic realities is, as we have seen, more central to the companion play, *King John*, than it is to *Richard II*, where, if it is opened, it is not really developed. Here the more essential concern is the loss of meaningful contact with the positive force that the past should have in the present and the fundamental problem this loss presents for the "new world" that tries to establish itself (as yet not very creatively) without the support of time's charters and customary rights. Fittingly, the character who both christens Henry's reign as "this new world" and swears by his intention to thrive in it is one of those petty wranglers whose partial versions of past events foster discord in it (IV, i, 78). If the play watches the whole process with an auspicious and a dropping eye, it is because it feels the potent appeal of the heroic heritage that is remembered sentimentally before fading out of view here and at the same time shares the realism of the new regime, even to the point of exposing the fissures that will shake that regime itself.[9] Those fissures are partly visible through the self-serving reconstructions of the past that destabilize the present and future. Only in the last play of the series that *Richard II* begins will Shakespeare offer a viable realization of the past's inspirational force that also fully acknowledges the fictive element in its history.

CHAPTER SIX

1 Henry IV

"Is Not the Truth the Truth?"

Unlike its more sober sequel, and unlike the first half of
Richard II, 1 Henry IV shows us an England that is no country
for old men or for their customary habit of retrospection.
The young in arms hold sway here, full of bright hope and
expectation:

> As full of spirit as the month of May
> And gorgeous as the sun at midsummer;
> Wanton as youthful goats, wild as young bulls.
>
> (IV, i, 101–103)

This is the description given to one "young Harry" of the other
and his comrades, and with crucial differences (including the

capacity to control and shape such descriptions) it fits both alike as they look ahead toward their climactic showdown at Shrewsbury. And looking ahead, youth's prerogative, is the play's dominant impulse, just as these two hopeful youths are the dominant forces in it. Both are lectured and cautioned by elders more subject to "care" who would curb what they perceive to be the errant wildness of the two young heroes. But the one young Harry needs no schooling and the other will brook none. They take their respective ways to Shrewsbury and carry all with them to victory and to defeat.

Even the elders in the play, sober and otherwise, catch and contribute to the play's spirit of anticipation. Henry himself (than whom none is more sober) opens the play, as he had closed *Richard II*, by looking ahead, not to what actually lies ahead but to the purgative crusade he hopes will "be commenced in stronds afar remote." His repeated "no more" is like an incantation designed to exorcise the turbulent legacy from the past that now bruises England "with the armèd hoofs / Of hostile paces." In his forward-looking mind's eye, Henry composes the present discord, "the intestine shock / And furious close of civil butchery," into an envisioned concord, where all Englishmen "shall now in mutual well-beseeming ranks / March all one way." That vision, as we shall see, will be achieved by Henry V by *awakening* memory rather than by denying it, as the shaken and wan king ("this forgetful man," as Hotspur later dubs him, not quite fairly) "bootless" tries to do here before yielding himself to present realities: "Therefor we meet not now." Among those grim realities, of course, Henry reckons a young foe "who is the theme of honor's tongue" and a son and heir whose brow is stained with riot and dishonor—"facts" which prompt this most pragmatic and toughminded of kings into one more brief flight of wishful fantasy about night-tripping fairies and changeling children before this first scene ends in a flurry of busy plans more suited to his council chamber.

Henry's sometime supporters and current antagonists, the rebel faction spearheaded by the Percies, are also a forward-looking lot, as we might expect rebels to be. "These promises are fair, the parties sure, / And our induction full of prosperous hope" (III, i, 2): that is not, as the student sweating through an identification quiz might reasonably guess, Hotspur speaking in his ever-onward vein but his temperate brother-in-law and co-conspirator, Mortimer. And their elder colleagues, too, are given to forecasts, couched in their own more circumspect terms:

> When time is ripe, which will be suddenly,
> I'll steal to Glendower and Lord Mortimer,
> Where you and Douglas, and our pow'rs at once,
> As I will fashion it, shall happily meet,
> To bear our fortunes in our own strong arms,
> Which now we hold at much uncertainty.
>
> (I, iii, 291–296)

The eldest of the play's principal characters shares the spirit of youthful expectation so fully that he dubs himself, in the heat of action, a youth indeed: "They hate us youth. Down with them! fleece them! . . . On, bacons, on! What, ye knaves! young men must live" (II, ii, 77–83). This is not, of course, the capacious Falstaff's only voice; but expectation shines in his opening sallies ("And I prithee, sweet wag, when thou art a king . . ." [I, ii, 14 ff.]), recurs as his continuing theme ("Rob me the exchequer the first thing thou doest" [III, iii, 175–176]), and attends his final exit ("If I do grow great, I'll grow less; for I'll purge, and leave sack, and live cleanly, as a nobleman should do" [V, iv, 159–161]).

No one, however, feels the future in the instant with such passionate intensity as Hotspur. He is, as he claims the rebel plot to be, "full of expectation" (II, iii, 17), and the Percy's cry of "Esperance" has for him peculiar force:

O, let the hours be short
Till fields and blows and groans applaud our sport!
                              (I, iii, 298–299)

I am on fire
To hear this rich reprisal is so nigh,
And yet not ours. Come, let me taste my horse,
Who is to bear me like a thunderbolt
Against the bosom of the Prince of Wales.
                              (IV, i, 117–121)

Whether at court, at home, in Wales, or in camp, Hotspur is
scarcely ever present but always straining ahead toward what he
will do. Wherever he may be until he finally faces Hal at Shrewsbury, "hot Lord Percy is," as Glendower says, "on fire to go"
(III, i, 261). Paradoxically, just as his activism finds vent in
verbal outbursts (though he "profess[es] not talking" [V, ii, 91],
he speaks more lines than any character save Falstaff), his impa-
tience to leap ahead sometimes hobbles whatever proceedings are
under way:

Imagination of some great exploit
Drives him beyond the bounds of patience.
.   .   .   .

He apprehends a world of figures here,
But not the form of what he should attend.
                              (I, iii, 199–210)

"Attending," in any sense of the word, doesn't suit Hotspur. And
when his imagination soars away, it characteristically soars ahead
to "some great exploit."

Though Hotspur's princely counterpart looks, by contrast with
this "theme of honor's tongue," so unlikely from his father's
limited vantage point, the capacities that favor the heir apparent
are perfectly clear in our more privileged view. Control fostered
by knowledge of himself and others, together with the ability to

use imagination rather than being driven by it, sets Hal off from (and over) a rival who, by his own admission, "cannot choose" how he behaves (III, i, 146). Hal's advantages have been frequently and thoroughly traced elsewhere with varying degrees of admiration and distaste, and rather than reviewing them here in full detail I will focus on them only as they emerge through the "expectation" that he shares with his eager antagonist.[1] Hal, like Hotspur, sets the play's sights forward toward its climax from his first appearance. But he does so with a characteristically acute sense of present circumstances and their relation to the future. For Hotspur, the present is something to be bypassed as swiftly as possible to reach the all-consuming but little-considered exploit he anticipates: "O, let the hours be short." Hal can not only bide his time, he can enjoy the interim while it ripens: "But Ned, to drive away the time till Falstaff come" (II, iv, 25–26). In such a lax moment, he can choose to let himself go rather than being driven willy-nilly by one compelling humor: "I am now of all humors that have showed themselves humors since the old days of goodman Adam to the pupil age of this present twelve o'clock at midnight" (89–91). And, even in the lull that allows him to place "this present" hour so humorously in the scopic context that began with Adam, he can anticipate (with easy irony rather than fiery urgency) the time when it will suit him to adopt Hotspur's militant mode: "I am not *yet* of Percy's mind, the Hotspur of the North" (97–98; emphasis added).

Most significantly for our purposes, as an extension of this clear-eyed placement of "now" in relation to then, Hal can foresee how the present will be perceived as past in the future. It is thus that he plans to frame his future action by the memory of what he has been and creatively shapes what will come to be the "story" of his past. This is the gist, of course, of the early soliloquy in which he previews for our benefit, with an accuracy granted no other forecaster in the play, his carefully planned "reformation." Not only "full of expectation," like his rival but with full awareness of how others' expectations may be dramatically reversed to his advantage, Hal "will awhile uphold" the humor (and his public image) of idleness to give his unlooked-for emergence maximum effect:

> So, when this loose behavior I throw off
> And pay the debt I never promisèd,
> By how much better than my word I am,
> By so much shall I falsify men's hopes;
> And, like bright metal on a sullen ground,
> My reformation, glitt'ring o'er my fault,
> Shall show more goodly and attract more eyes
> Than that which hath no foil to set it off.
> I'll so offend to make offense a skill,
> Redeeming time when men think least I will.
>
> (I, ii, 196–205)

Here Shakespeare's history gives us a privileged (and necessarily fictive) view of Hal consciously creating what others, less fully informed than we are, will suppose to be the "history" of his reformation. Implicit in this soliloquy may be the creative understanding of history that the prince will later display and employ as Henry V. But, for whatever reasons, despite all his evident intellectual reach and easy range of reference, Hal never calls on history at all in *1 Henry IV*. He will "imitate the sun" (185), but he looks to no predecessor for a model, nor does he make any other use of the past. As far as he is concerned in this play, his "story," over which he exercises such deft control, begins with his own wayward youth, his delinquency as heir apparent.[2]

Curiously, it is Hotspur, that least reflective and most headlong of heroes, who recites more history than any other character in *1 Henry IV*. And curiously, in doing so, this fervid devotee of heroic militancy cites no historical model, no glorious predecessor whose spirit he will emulate or revive, though he knows that what "men of nobility and power" do will "fill up chronicles in time to come" either to their shame or glory (I, iii, 170–187). Or perhaps not so curiously after all—for what noble precedent might he evoke for rebellion that pushes against the kingdom to "o'erturn it topsy-turvy down" (IV, i, 81–82)? In any case, neither he nor anyone else here looks back to an ancestral model for his action, save when "poor Jack Falstaff" cites Adam's precedent for his own fleshy frailty (III, iii, 157–161). *1 Henry IV* is unique among the plays of the second tetralogy (indeed, in the entire series of histories) in its total abstinence from any recollection of the valiant dead, any evocation of heroic forebears whatsoever—a fact that may be all the more surprising since it is the only play of the series to be structured on the contest between two such attractive aspirants to heroic glory.

There may be a reason more fundamental than Hotspur's questionable cause or Hal's original course why no such positive use of historical models is made in this play—a reason that coincides with Hotspur's odd eminence as "historian" in it. In Hotspur's hasty hands, as we might expect, the past, or his memory of it, is transmuted with unthinking swiftness to suit the mood that impels him forward against "this vile politician, Bolingbroke" (I, iii, 240). If Henry is seen as "this thorn, this canker," then by a "natural" (and certainly *not* considered) rhetorical process the dead Richard II becomes "that sweet lovely rose" (175–176). If we remember young Harry Percy's ready subservience to the returning Bolingbroke in Act II, scene iii of *Richard II* (or his father's oozing "good words" to Bolingbroke in that same scene), it certainly confirms our sense of Hotspur's selective memory of their encounter: "Why, what a candy deal of courtesy / This fawning greyhound then did proffer me!" (249–250). But we need not rely heavily on our own surer memories to see Hotspur's recollection working its ready adaptations to his new cause. Like the strongly colored terms of his account of these earlier events, both in I, iii to his own party and in IV, iii to Blunt, his later review of the rebellion's inception in this play itself shows his blatant bias. I am not saying, of course, that this headstrong young man lies, as his uncle will lie to him about the king's offer of "grace," or that he consciously reconstructs events in Falstaff's way. He simply sees as he so intensely feels, with no intimation (or memory) of anything that might modify or contradict his feeling (and hence his firm belief) about what is right.

Such a passion-filtered and personally slanted view of things past and present is precisely what we should expect from Hotspur. But Shakespeare is not thereby contrasting him here with other characters and their ways of recollecting. Rather, by giving Hotspur the featured place among "historians" in the play, he emphasizes (for Hotspur is nothing if not emphatic) the factor common to all recollections here, whatever variations may individualize them. All are conveniently colored by whatever lens happens to fit the beholder's eye—each more pointedly so in juxtaposition with the others, but each self-evidently so in itself. Thus Worcester, with more self-consciousness and cynicism, surely, recites to Henry the Percified version of the rebellion that makes it somehow all Henry's doing—essentially the same story of abused innocence that Hotspur had recounted to Blunt:

> We were enforced for safety sake to fly
> Out of your sight and raise this present head;
> Whereby we stand opposèd by such means
> As you yourself have forged against yourself
> By unkind usage, dangerous countenance,
> And violation of all faith and troth
> Sworn to us in your younger enterprise.
>
> (V, i, 65–71)

Henry can counter such a partial, self-serving account by accurately describing how its decorative facade takes its shape and color:

> These things, indeed, you have articulate,
> Proclaimed at market crosses, read in churches,
> To face the garment of rebellion
> With some fine color that may please the eye.

.   .   .   .

And never yet did insurrection want
Such water colors to impaint his cause.

(72–80)

But he cannot (or does not) counter it with a more credibly comprehensive history of the events Worcester and Hotspur remember so partially. Not only does he share the rebels' convenient
habit of disclaiming any responsibility for the deadly conflict
under way ("You have deceived our trust / And *made* us doff our
easy robes of peace / To crush our old limbs in ungentle steel"
[V, i, 11–13; emphasis added]); he also shares their capacity for
reconstructing the past in the most self-gratifying terms, using his
own "water colors to impaint" his own cause. According to Hotspur, Bolingbroke skulked back to England virtually unnoticed
till Northumberland, out of pure charity, adopted him and simply
gave him all the public countenance he ever gained:

My father and my uncle and myself
Did give him that same royalty he wears;
And when he was not six-and-twenty strong,
Sick in the world's regard, wretched and low,
A poor unminded outlaw sneaking home,
My father gave him welcome to the shore;
And when he heard him swear and vow to God
He came but to be Duke of Lancaster,
To sue his livery and beg his peace,
With tears of innocency and terms of zeal,
My father, in kind heart and pity moved,
Swore him assistance, and performed it too.
Now when the lords and barons of the realm
Perceived Northumberland did lean to him,
The more and less came in with cap and knee;
Met him in boroughs, cities, villages,
Attended him on bridges, stood in lanes,
Laid gifts before him, proffered him their oaths,

Gave him their heirs as pages, followed him
Even at the heels in golden multitudes.

(IV, iii, 54–73)

Henry, as we have seen, would prefer to forget the more immediate past and its troubles if he could, looking ahead instead toward the *ignis fatuus* of his holy crusade. But he does look back
fondly to that lustrous time when he "from France set foot at
Ravenspurgh" and proceeded to win the hearts and minds of the
people by his own decorously staged campaign, with no remembered help from the unmentioned Percies:

By being seldom seen, I could not stir
But, like a comet, I was wond'red at;
That men would tell their children, "This is he!"
Others would say, "Where? Which is Bolingbroke?"
And then I stole all courtesy from heaven,
And dressed myself in such humility
That I did pluck allegiance from men's hearts,
Loud shouts and salutations from their mouths
Even in the presence of the crownèd king.
Thus did I keep my person fresh and new,
My presence, like a robe pontifical,
Ne'er seen but wond'red at; and so my state,
Seldom but sumptuous, showed like a feast
And wan by rareness such solemnity.

(III, ii, 95, 46–59)

How, then, did Bolingbroke ascend to such regal stature in
men's eyes? Was it his doing or Northumberland's? It depends,
of course, on whom you ask.[3]

Biased and mutually contradictory recollections are not in and
of themselves new phenomena in the histories. From the earliest
plays in the series, old Mortimer and his eager protégé bolstered
the Yorkist cause with anti-Lancastrian surveys that were rhetorically slanted, however genealogically correct. Behind those plays,

however, and fully embedded in the first of them, stood a solid heritage of English history, attested to even by the enemy French and their countryman Froissart (*1HVI*, I, ii, 29–36). As the factious nobles lost sight of that heritage, that was to their discredit and the nation's detriment, but the sense of the past they *should* have honored and emulated suffered, in itself, no discredit or doubt. Nor does *Richard III* prompt anyone, onstage or off, to question the awful truth of the recent past that haunts its "hero" and his stricken world. And the memory of a better time clings to its survivors through the first half of *Richard II*. As we have seen, that perhaps idealized but clearly positive memory gives way in the second half of that play to the evidently self-serving and conflicting memories of those who "intend to thrive in this new world" of Henry Bolingbroke (IV, i, 78). What distinguishes *1 Henry IV* from its predecessors is that such obviously "impainted" recollections are the only kind in it. The remembered past becomes a baseless fabric, woven in the clashing colors of opposed visions. Nor does the play itself offer any assurance of a "truer" history that could be seen through some more dependable lens than a Hotspur's or a Henry's eye. In some instances, to be sure, we can match our own experience of dramatized events (whether here or in *Richard II*) against a character's account of them, and in one notorious instance we can thus verify the "plain tale" that exposes gross and palpable lies. But we are not—and cannot be—always so privileged. No one, as the narrator of Chaucer's *Legend of Good Women* ingenuously remarks to open his prologue, sees everything. So what are we to believe when, to use a less ingenuous commentator's terms, no one sees and nothing could confute (or verify) but eyes? When, for example, Henry categorically denies Hotspur's glowing account of an epic encounter we did not witness between Mortimer and Glendower on Severn's sedgy banks?

Though he sometimes subjects himself to our eyes' confutation of his grand fabrications, Falstaff's large presence nonetheless comically punctuates the unreliability of all reporters and their recollections in the play. His sportive fictions, playfully pointing even as they blossom to their own absurdity, also underscore how ubiquitously this world is given, if not to lying, at least to reconstructing its memories to suit themselves. We would scarcely credit Henry or Hotspur or Worcester at their own estimates anyway, but Falstaff's fabulous contrivances cast a more ironically amusing light on their solemn constructions of things after their respective fashions. Moreover, Falstaff's recollections point up the fact that others' references to the past come only in the form of such purposive constructions, and that no one else in this play makes any gesture toward the heroic heritage that had inspired current action or contrasted with current woes in previous histories. The image of a glorious past to be awakened, or that is being shamefully neglected, is simply not offered seriously in any form in this play. It emerges only in the grotesque shapes that Falstaff's comic conjurations of lost virtue—his own or the world's at large—give to it:

> Go thy ways, old Jack, die when thou wilt; if manhood,
> good manhood, be not forgot upon the face of the earth,
> then I am a shotten herring. There lives not three good
> men unhanged in England; and one of them is fat, and
> grows old. God help the while! A bad world, I say.
> (II, iv, 119–124)

That this sentiment survives only in such terms and on such scarce-wiped lips naturally subverts here whatever credit a Gaunt or a York had lent it. *Richard II* allowed us some sympathetic skepticism about these elders' idealizing memories but also allowed their recollected ideal to stand in positive contrast to personalized reconstructions of the past that fostered civil conflict. In *1 Henry IV*, apart from Falstaff's parodic nostalgia, the past is recalled exclusively through such reconstructions.[4]

The play should not, however, be cast as a darkly skeptical essay in historical relativism. It is more buoyed by hope than weighted by retrospection, and we are invited to enjoy (at least as much as to ponder) the fiery spirit with which Hotspur pursues his hope and the high spirits with which Hal first bides and then seizes his time. Nonetheless, in the context I have been developing, the fact that neither of these heroic young aspirants evokes any historical model seems all the more striking. It is risky business to guess what might have been the case were the play written otherwise than it is, but we might wonder how such models would fare, especially if Hotspur called on them, in a play where every recollection is so suspect, so patently geared to the needs or desires of the recollector. In any case, we can see clearly enough how the only application made in the play of models from the past misfires in this context. When Henry, no high all-seer, gives Hal in earnest the lecture that Falstaff had rehearsed in jest, he casts Hal and Hotspur in the roles that Richard and he had played when his own sun was rising:

> For all the world,
> As thou art to this hour was Richard then
> When I from France set foot at Ravenspurgh;
> And even as I was then is Percy now.
>
> (III, ii, 93–96)

No alert audience can miss the irony here as Henry (less advantaged than we in viewpoint) misses the actual correspondence between Hal's current control and his own remembered control over developing perceptions of their "sunlike majesty," and as he misses the radical difference between his own calculated behavior then, as he describes it, and the rash impetuosity of the Hotspur, with whom he oddly identifies himself now. And yet, however incongruous the ways of Henry's policy and Hotspur's chivalry may seem when distilled into their antithetical characters, Hal, now playing out his pre-scripted reformation, *does* manage to combine in himself both of these qualities, thereby making his father's didactic mangle of apparently conflicting models (Henry himself and Hotspur) more coherent than it has any inherent right to be.

But if Hal, when the occasion suits him, can adapt Hotspur's model to his purposes—can "play Percy" (II, iv, 104)—it is clearly to his advantage that he does not simply model himself after his rival or "become" a very Hotspur, as his father wistfully wishes he might in the first scene and again in the paternal lecture at midplay. How far the ironies of that lecture extend to the "never-dying honor" Henry there attributes to Hotspur (106) is not a simple question, and full consideration of it would involve a careful estimate of the interplay between Falstaff's bulky shadow and the "bright honor" to which Hotspur so fervently commits himself (I, iii, 202). We need not pursue the question that far, however, to see that Hotspur's headlong commitment fares ill in a world of politic Bolingbrokes, lying Worcesters, tedious Glendowers, and ailing Northumberlands. He is overmatched by a prince who can emulate his valor but whose other dimensions are simply beyond his ken. He surely is, as Hal praises him for being, as "active-valiant" and as "valiant-young" as any "now alive / To grace this latter age with noble deeds" (V, i, 89–92). But "this latter age," or "this new world," will demand more from a leader than such gallant activism, however vibrant and attractive it may be in a youth who is "the theme of honor's tongue."[5]

All this is patent enough. What is of focal interest to our topic here, however we gauge the play's estimate of honor's value and viability in "this latter age," is the firm limit placed on the sense in which Hotspur's honor might be "never-dying," as the king says it is. For if the play recalls no dead hero, it ends with the death of this young hero at Hal's more capable (and equally heroic) hands. And Hal is explicit about the ways in which Hotspur's honor will and will not survive, and about what he will and will not revive in his own person from this now lost leader who had been held up to him as a model. There is a marked contrast with such an earlier tribute and commitment to the "valiant dead" as that given by Talbot over the fallen Salisbury (1HVI, I, iv), though of course the fact that Hotspur is a fallen foe and rebel accounts for much of the difference. Granted the different circum-

stance, the way in which the prince intends to incorporate the
honor of the fallen hero in his own person here both recalls the
earlier transferral from the dead to the living leader and reveals
other important differences in its nature. Talbot had identified
himself with the dying Salisbury, whose very spirit he will maintain for the present and memorialize for the future: "Frenchmen,
I'll be a Salisbury to you" (106). Hal had invoked that simpler,
clearer idea of incorporating the spirit of the valiant dead just
once, and briefly, as he confronted the Douglas in the heat of
battle: "The spirits / Of valiant Shirley, Stafford, Blunt are in mine
arms." But even there it was his own identity, now "breaking
through" as planned from "the foul and ugly mists / Of vapors
that did seem to strangle him" (I, ii, 190–191), that he insisted
upon: "It is the Prince of Wales that threatens thee, / Who never
promiseth but he means to pay" (V, iv, 41–42). And when he
pays exactly what he had earlier promised his anxious father by
vanquishing Percy, the terms of the transfer of honor from Hotspur to Hal are not those in which Talbot had given new life to
the spirit of dead Salisbury. Hal generously praises the size of
Hotspur's spirit when it was living, and "a kingdom for it was
too small a bound." And, now that its earthly embodiment is
food for worms, he generously allows that spirit's praise to ascend
to heaven, consigning its ignominy to the grave. But there is no
question of reviving and continuing Percy's spirit in his own
person as a historical legacy to be passed on. Hal will, rather,
as he had promised, *appropriate* the honor that Hotspur had
hitherto won:

> Percy is but my factor, good my lord,
> To engross up glorious deeds on my behalf.
>
> (III, ii, 147–148)

> I am the Prince of Wales, and think not, Percy,
> To share with me in glory any more.

.   .   .   .

And all the budding honors on thy crest
I'll crop to make a garland for my head.

(V, iv, 62–72)

Insofar as Hotspur's honor lives on, it lives now as Hal's, with no
"share" left for the dead rival. To this extent only does the prince
perpetuate his legacy from Percy. No more than he had recalled
or revived any past model will Hotspur himself continue to live
as an inspiring memory. If his soaring spirit helped to buoy the
atmosphere of this lively play, it serves, as we shall see, no vitalizing purpose after his death in the dramatized future of the sequel.
Nor does the future leader, as he himself seems to know, have
anything to gain or carry forward from his dead rival, save the
glory he crops by defeating him.[6]

That glory serves Hal's own "story," which will become part of
the perceived history he alone foresees. Though it is not an untrue
story (Hal needs no lie to do him grace), we are allowed nonetheless to see the gap between the full truth and the fiction of it that
the prince consciously crafts for public consumption. But Hal as
yet does not openly extend to the larger reach of recorded history
the understanding of true fiction that we will share with him in
Henry V. For all the promising notes it sounds, this history play's
"latter age" dramatizes for us no positive model of the use of history, which appears in it only in the watercolors with which the
various partisans impaint their causes. And that impulse, even at
its most "innocent" and insistent in a Hotspur, finally offers
nothing substantial enough to survive the "cold hand of death"
lying on the tongue that gave it voice (V, iv, 82–83).

CHAPTER SEVEN

2 Henry IV

"What Perils Past, What Crosses to Ensue"

Retrospection, as we have seen, is a major concern throughout the histories. Even where it is minimal in a character (Richard II) or in a play (*2 and 3 Henry VI*), its very absence is significant. And through most of the series, characters look back as often and with as wide a variety of moods and motives as they look ahead. As the archbishop of York suggests, much of the time "past and to come seems best, things present worst" (I, iii, 108).[1] Yet *2 Henry IV* stands out in this context both as an emphatically retrospective play and as one in which memory is largely oppressive or futile or (as in Part One) faulty. And despite the archbishop's even-handed distribution of the superlative to past and future alike (an attitude that he attributes scornfully, whether justly or not, to the "vulgar heart"), scarcely anyone in this autumnal play casts the future in bright colors or looks eagerly ahead.

The contrast with the youthful and hopeful mood of Part One is a sharp one. Here, rather than springing eternal in rebel breasts, hope becomes the subject of their anxious debate as they edge themselves dubiously toward confrontation (I, iii). Others seem to dread the future they foresee. The king shapes "in forms imaginary the unguided days / And rotten times" to come when "the fifth Harry from curbed license plucks / The muzzle of restraint" (IV, iv, 58–60; v, 128–132). Even the prince, for all his firm resolve, speaks of his royal future in terms of the weight that will descend on him with the crown, not of the sun that will burst forth, as he once had done (IV, iv, 20–42). Hope only flares up in full force once, as Falstaff and his eager cohorts gallop toward the coronation, and we watch with full awareness that this brief flame will be thoroughly extinguished, even if the sudden chill of the new king's response to his old friend still shocks us.

As hope dwindles to a hollow jingle in Pistol's rusty repertoire ("sperato me contento") and as no one finds a good word for "these costermongers' times" themselves (I, ii, 161), only memories of the past glow warmly in any among the weary, the ailing, and the aged who are prominently featured in this play. Though the elegiac note sounds at Justice Shallow's Gloucestershire establishment in the psalmist's plaintive certainty that "all shall die" as old Double has, the complacency of rural business-as-usual that rubs shoulders so easily with this lament and the singular sense of well-being that prevails here as nowhere else in this play's "old world" are voiced in Shallow's entirely self-gratifying version of *ubi sunt*. Dead Double shines along with the craft's master of the Mile-end drill squad ("I shall ne'er see such a fellow") in Shallow's rosy memory:

> 'A drew a good bow, and dead! 'A shot a fine shoot. John a
> Gaunt loved him well and betted much money on his head.

Dead! 'A would have clapped i' the clout at twelve score,
and carried you a forehand shaft a fourteen and fourteen
and a half, that it would have done a man's heart good to
see. How a score of ewes now? (III, ii, 39–47)

Only the slender figure of the young justice-to-be himself is
coddled more fondly in Shallow's recollection of his Inns o' Court
exploits and "the feats he hath done about Turnbull Street":
"Jesus, the days that we have seen!" (261–286, 207).

Our view of this mellow memory is, of course, ironic—if more
gently so than Falstaff's, all the more clearly so for that witness's
shrewd testimony that every third word the justice utters is a lie:

I do remember him at Clement's Inn like a man made after
supper of a cheese-paring. When 'a was naked, he was, for
all the world, like a forked radish, with a head fantastically
carved upon it with a knife. 'A was so forlorn that his dimensions to any thick sight were invincible. 'A was the
very genius of famine, yet lecherous as a monkey, and the
whores called him mandrake. 'A came ever in the rearward
of the fashion, and sung those tunes to the overscutched
huswives that he heard the carmen whistle, and sware they
were his fancies or his good-nights. And now is this Vice's
dagger become a squire, and talks as familiarly of John a
Gaunt as he had been sworn brother to him, and I'll be
sworn 'a ne'er saw him but once in the Tilt-yard, and then
he burst his head for crowding among the marshal's men.
(287–301)

This reduction of the already insubstantial Shallow places idealization of the past in a very different light here than was afforded
it in *Richard II*. If York then magnified the exploits of "noble
Edward's sons" in memory, no sardonic commentator stood by to
tell us so. However ineffectual that aged duke's actions might have
seemed in the "new world" of Bolingbroke's ascendancy, his recollections of a better, more heroic past stood as a clear and posi-

tive (though perhaps varnished) model against which the fallen present's troubles could be measured. And just as the credit given to such nostalgia evaporates when York's role is assumed by Shallow, so general reflection on the decline and fall of past grandeur shrinks from Gaunt's deathbed vision to Falstaff's banter in the streets:

> Virtue is of so little regard in these costermongers' times that true valor is turned bearherd. Pregnancy is made a tapster, and hath his quick wit wasted in giving reckonings. All the other gifts appertinent to man, as the malice of this age shapes them, are not worth a gooseberry. (I, ii, 160–165)

As we have seen, Falstaff also struck this nostalgic chord occasionally in *1 Henry IV*. If it sounds more often in Part Two (and mostly in Gloucestershire), it is given no more credit and certainly no more positive vitality. In this play's melancholy world, even Edward III, that heroic sire of seven fair branches, is recalled on the authority of "the old folk, time's doting chronicles" only as a precedent for unnatural omens foretelling a king's death, not as a model for emulation (IV, iv, 121–128). That the past seems best is, according to the archbishop of York, a function of "thoughts of men accursed," not a viable truth or even a valuable fiction. And those memories in *2 Henry IV* that are not comically subverted, as Shallow's are, seem cursed and tormented indeed. Most tormented of all are those of the ailing king. Glowing images of his glory days, when his "person [was] fresh and new" and his "presence, like a robe pontifical, / Ne'er seen but wond'red at," no longer brighten his remembrance (*1HIV*, III, ii, 50–59). His uneasy head swims, rather, with such recollections as that of Richard's telling prophecy to Northumberland, the truth of which, now seen in retrospect, prompts Henry's nihilistic pronouncement on the book of fate and the revolution of the times.[2] To see the latter truly would kill any spirit (III, i, 45–79). No quitter, for all that, Henry will meet necessities for what they are when they confront him (92–94). But he confronts the past less courageously, fobbing his usurpation off on necessity itself ("God knows, I had no such intent, / But that necessity so bowed the state / That I and greatness were compelled to kiss" [72–74]) and, even at the last, referring any true knowledge of his "bypaths and indirect crooked ways" to God alone (IV, v, 184). When memory is so troubling to the king, both in his own mind and in the minds of those still "living to upbraid" the "gain" he achieved with their assistance, it is small wonder that he would blot it out if he could (192–193). And so we hear him urge his son toward what will be the glory of Agincourt, not in the likeness of heroic models whose deeds at Crécy and Poitiers live in memory, and not with the purpose of reviving that former time's greatness, but with the precisely opposite motive of erasing the past and its problems:

> Therefore, my Harry,
> Be it thy course to busy giddy minds
> With foreign quarrels, that action, hence borne out,
> May *waste the memory of the former days*.
> (212–215; emphasis added)

In fact, in this play where the single staged battle features John of Lancaster's nasty deception of the faltering rebels, no one in the deadly serious overplot ever recalls a past hero to inspire a present one. Citation of heroic prototypes serves no more exalted cause than Pistol's rant ("Shall pack-horses / And hollow pampered jades of Asia, / Which cannot go but thirty mile a-day, / Compare with Caesars, and with Cannibals, / And Trojan Greeks?" [II, iv, 148–152]), Doll's praise ("Come on, you whoreson chops. . . . Thou art as valorous as Hector of Troy, worth five of Agamemnon, and ten times better than the Nine Worthies" [201–205]), or Falstaff's wit ("I may justly say, with the hook-nosed fellow of Rome, their Caesar, 'I came, saw, and overcame'" [IV, iii, 39–41]).[3] The thesis for positive use of past experience is advanced only in Warwick's pragmatic terms:

> There is a history in all men's lives,
> Figuring the nature of the times deceased,
> The which observed, a man may prophesy,
> With a near aim, of the main chance of things
> As yet not come to life, which in their seeds
> And weak beginnings lie intreasurèd.
>
> (III, i, 80–85)

In practice, such analytic prophesying (which we saw at work in Pandulph's common craft and in Richard II's singular foresight) is not a sure science by which to steer one's course here, as the archbishop finds when he correctly computes Henry's wish to "wipe his tables clean / And keep no tell-tale to his memory / That may repeat and history his loss / To new remembrance" (IV, i, 201–204), and then, on that apparently firm basis, steps straight into the Lancastrian trap. And of course Hal's planned reformation is designed to foil any such calculation from past behavior—"to mock the expectation of the world" (V, ii, 126)—and therefore takes Warwick and his theory by surprise.[4]

In this play, then, introduced as it is by the unsettling spirit of Rumor, the remembrance of things past is given little positive thrust.[5] It is patently false, or painfully true, or provides slippery ground upon which to proceed. It also serves, as in Part One, as an open text for contrary interpretations when the rebels parley with the king's forces, though here the futility of such debate is even more immediately underscored as Mowbray and Westmoreland stray into pointless speculation about what *would* have happened *if* Richard had not aborted the trial by combat at Coventry (IV, i, 125–139). Memory serves its single positive purpose in Part Two, as it had in Part One, in the prince's creative use of it as he once again carries out his plan to redeem the time when men least think he will. That plan depends, of course, on sustaining the memory of his former "riot," by contrast with his father's need to "waste the memory of the former days." Thus, once crowned, he immediately forces his earlier infamous encounter with the lord chief justice into public view ("May this be washed in Lethe, and forgotten?") so that his staged reformation can shine against its proper foil and "raze out / Rotten opinion," rather than razing out recollection, as his father would have him do (V, ii, 68–145). But even the perfectly successful manipulation of "opinion" has its heavy undertow for Hal, whose keynote in this play is weariness (II, ii, 1). The role in which he has cast himself now controls him as much as he controls it, so that he cannot show his true grief over his father's illness without confounding the "opinion" he is cultivating (36–59). And his future role as the "true" prince will demand as careful control of his own memory as of others' memories. "What a disgrace it is to me," he says to Poins, reflecting on the role his "greatness" demands of him, "to remember thy name," let alone to "remember the poor creature, small beer" (10–14). When he "reforms," he will not allow himself such a disgrace. No evident flicker of memory mars his stern approval when, in the next play, "one Pardolph" is executed for robbing a French cross (*HV*, III, vi, 97–104). And though, at this play's end, he may "have long dreamed of such a kind of man," he is not so disgraced as to remember Falstaff's name: "I know thee not, old man" (V, v, 48–50). That harsh pronouncement takes the edge off whatever pleasure attends the fulfillment of our expectations—the only expectations (besides Hal's own) that are likely to have survived unscathed through the host of discouragements cataloged by various parties in the play. And the reflective prince's remarks to Poins, whose lack of such disturbing reflection Hal professes to envy for the moment ("Thou art a blessed fellow to think as every man thinks" [II, ii, 51–52]), suggest the price he himself pays for such purposive forgetfulness. No more than the "victory" at Gaultree does this success have the zest and exhilaration with which the young prince vaulted toward his first showdown at Shrewsbury (*1HIV*, IV, i, 104–110).

The absence in Part Two of the vibrant spirit that buoyed Part One, evident in every aspect of the play touched on thus far, is nowhere felt more keenly than in the absence of that spirit's very incarnation, Harry Percy, the Hotspur of the North. With his absence we come to our particular focus, for he is the lost leader remembered here. And with the remembrance of Hotspur, the figure of the lost leader reaches its nadir in the histories. In the dispirited atmosphere of 2 *Henry IV*, instead of providing inspiration for renewal, the dead hero turns into a dead end.

The heroic note on which the play proper opens with news of Hotspur's happy victory is, as we already know when Lord Bardolph sounds it, a false one, blown on Rumor's windy pipe:

> O, such a day,
> So fought, so followed, and so fairly won,
> Came not till now to dignify the times
> Since Caesar's fortunes!
>
> (I, i, 20–23)

Northumberland tries briefly to sustain this lofty mode as he anticipates the truth in Morton's grim countenance:

> Even such a man, so faint, so spiritless,
> So dull, so dead in look, so woebegone,
> Drew Priam's curtain in the dead of night,
> And would have told him half his Troy was burnt.
> But Priam found the fire ere he his tongue.
>
> (70–74)

But despite Morton's own effort to soften his blow by answering in terms that would keep Northumberland thus elevated ("You are too great to be by me gainsaid. / Your spirit is too true, your fears too certain" [91–92]), all such allusions placing the present action on a level with ancient archetypes drop from the overplot and fall, as we have seen, to the likes of Pistol.

Once the true story of Shrewsbury is out, Morton offers two apparently contradictory retrospective views of Hotspur's effectiveness as a living leader. The second is intended rhetorically to bolster Northumberland's faith in the archbishop of York's surviving chances to "turn insurrection to religion," and so the invidious comparison made at Hotspur's expense cannot be taken as Morton's straight assessment of the latter's inspirational value as a hero. The contrast with Talbot is nonetheless telling. Whereas that exemplar had styled himself "but a shadow" whose true "substance, sinews, arms, and strength" consisted in the soldiers he led so winningly (*1HVI*, II, iii, 60–66), Hotspur "had only but the corpse, / But shadows and the shows of men, to fight" (192–193). True, it is their cause and not their leader that freezes the spirits of Hotspur's followers. Talbot's men are the force "with which he yoketh . . . rebellious [French] necks" (64), whereas "that same word 'rebellion' did divide" the bodies from the souls of Hotspur's troops. At best, in any event, and in the more positive terms of Morton's earlier account, it was only while he lived that Hotspur's "spirit lent a fire / Even to the dullest peasant in his camp." His death, "being bruited once, took fire and heat away / From the best-tempered courage in his troops. / For from his metal was his party steeled, / Which once in him abated, all the rest / Turned on themselves, like dull and heavy lead" (112–118). No one picks up the torch, as Talbot had done when Salisbury died ("Frenchmen, I'll be a Salisbury to you" [*1HVI*, I, iv, 106]). We scarcely expect so much from the "dullest peasant," to be sure, but even the "bloody Douglas," a likely enough heroic successor to the fallen Percy, "did grace the shame / Of those that turned their backs, and in his flight, / Stumbling in fear, was took" (127–131).

With Hotspur's death, then, the fire simply went out. It may seem to rekindle briefly in his father when the old earl hears this "news at full," but only as the last frenzied flare of a "wretch whose fever-weakened joints, / Like strengthless hinges, buckle under life" (140–141). In that "fit," the "enraged Northumberland" neither calls on the spirit of his son nor avows any renewal of Hotspur's heroic example in his own person or in a phoenix to be reared hereafter. Instead, he invokes the all-destructive "spirit of the first-born Cain" to "reign in all bosoms, that, each heart being set / On bloody courses, the rude scene may end, / And darkness be the burier of the dead!" (157–160). Northumberland here anticipates the nihilistic outbursts of Lear and Macbeth, and by that dismal light the contrast with Talbot's or Lucy's impulse to keep the hero's memory alive by emulation now and in the future shows itself to be absolute:

> Let heaven kiss earth! Now let not Nature's hand
> Keep the wild flood confined! Let order die!
> And let this world no longer be a stage
> To feed contention in a lingering act.
>
> (153–156)[6]

The old earl also echoes, in his extremity, the fury of young Clifford at his father's death:

> O, let the vile world end
> And the premisèd flames of the last day
> Knit earth and heaven together.
> (2*HVI*, V, ii, 40–42)

But, after all, Northumberland's "fit" *is* only a feverish sputter, and he subsides quickly into the absurdly oxymoronic posture of a cautious Clifford: "Go in with me, and counsel every man / The aptest way for safety and revenge" (212–213). This "crafty-sick" elder retains none of the passionate intensity that fuels Clifford's fury and Lear's tragic vision. As he retires into his "worm-eaten hold of ragged stone" to take counsel, he enacts, in effect, the expiration of the fiery spirit of Hotspur that has been this scene's principal subject and that makes of it an apt introduction to the play's sober history. "Of Hotspur Coldspur" (50). The epitaph epitomizes the way in which this hero's death quenches whatever inspirational force he may have had in life.

Hotspur is recalled twice more early in the play, and both instances further deny any positive recreative spirit to his memory.

First, and most simply, he is used as a negative example in the rebels' debate about the wisdom of proceeding on the supposition that Northumberland will reinforce them:

> *Lord Bard.*: For in a theme so bloody-faced as this,
> Conjecture, expectation, and surmise
> Of aids incertain should not be admitted.
> *Archbishop*: 'Tis very true, Lord Bardolph, for indeed
> It was young Hotspur's case at Shrewsbury.
> *Lord Bard.*: It was, my lord, who lined himself with hope,
> Eating the air on promise of supply,
> Flattering himself in project of a power
> Much smaller than the smallest of his thoughts,
> And so, with great imagination
> Proper to madmen, led his powers to death
> And winking leaped into destruction.
>
> (I, iii, 22–33)

We might recall, by contrast, the glowing tribute paid by Lucy to Talbot after that hero "leaped into destruction" in circumstances not dissimilar.[7]

If his own allies ("our friends true and constant, . . . good friends, and full of expectation, . . . very good friends" [*1HIV*, II, iii, 15–17]) thus reduce the theme of honor's tongue to a hare-brained Hotspur governed by spleen, his widow's treatment of his memory is more curious and more complex. She recalls him, as we would hope she might, at his own best estimate. Just as Talbot hailed the dying Salisbury as the "mirror of all martial men" (*1HVI*, I, iv, 74), so Lady Percy remembers her husband as "the glass / Wherein the noble youth did dress themselves" and dwells in full detail on his exemplary force, his power to inspire emulation in others:

> And by his light
> Did all the chivalry of England move
> To do brave acts. He was indeed the glass

Wherein the noble youth did dress themselves.
He had no legs that practiced not his gait;
And speaking thick, which nature made his blemish,
Became the accents of the valiant,
For those that could speak low and tardily
Would turn their own perfection to abuse,
To seem like him. So that in speech, in gait,
In diet, in affections of delight,
In military rules, humors of blood,
He was the mark and glass, copy and book,
That fashioned others.

(II, iii, 19–32)

Then, having thus recalled him, she uses her evocation of this
"miracle of men" to dissuade Northumberland from fulfilling
his pledge "to do brave acts" according to "military rules" in behalf of his allies and to prompt, instead, his own skin-saving
inclination to head for the border rather than the battlefield.
We can understand the lady's human motives for arguing that
Northumberland would do his son's "ghost . . . wrong" if he were
to hold his "honor more precise and nice / With others" than he
had with Hotspur himself. But Hotspur's ghost must writhe at
such a plea. Everything to which he had lent himself so single-
mindedly is violated thereby, and his widow's pledge "to rain
upon remembrance" with her eyes "that it may grow and sprout
as high as heaven, / For recordation to . . . [her] noble husband"
(59–61) thus loses any meaning he might have understood or
appreciated. Lady Percy here makes the only gesture toward keeping Hotspur's memory alive in the play (and in the future), and
she does so in a way that thwarts the pursuit of his heroic example. Whatever faint spark of honor might have lingered in
Northumberland's chilly breast fizzles out under her dissuasion:
"Fair daughter, you do draw my spirits from me" (46). That is
scarcely the way to renew the feats of the valiant dead. And, with

that, all "recordation" of Harry Hotspur disappears from view. He is never mentioned again in this play or its sequel.

The sequel belongs to Hotspur's rival, and the reasons why Hal succeeds where Hotspur and others fail are apparent enough. Fighting in a questionable cause that he himself does not have understanding enough to question, Hotspur has more strikes against him than the fact that he is an outmoded hero whose beliefs and ways cannot cope with "this new world." But it is not only the familiar distinction between the qualities of these two heroes themselves, "old" and "new," that is my concern here. Uppermost among those qualities, of course, is the fuller awareness that allows one man to redeem the time by using it while the other remains time's fool. A larger awareness than Hal's, however, shapes our understanding of both heroes and, by placing them in such different retrospective patterns, suggests the different possibilities of historical perspective as well as showing us two very different kinds of leaders.

The denial of any recreative potential to the memory of Hotspur, though it may be a particular function of the limitations of that hero himself and of those who remember him, is also symptomatic of a play in which the past, in all its varied *presence*, weighs heavily as a stifling burden rather than offering recreative inspiration. Nor are we offered the presumably uplifting reassurance that places the past's burden under the precise supervision of that high All-seer who meted out retribution in *Richard III*. There is about this play, rather, with its dominantly aged set of characters, a spirit of weary disillusion that afflicts even the young prince. Even the happiest youth, according to Henry's reflection on "the revolution of the times," would, if his illusions about the course of things were destroyed, "sit him down and die" (III, i, 45–79). Such a pale cast of thought, if submitted to, is more profoundly paralyzing than Northumberland's brief flirtation with destructive frenzy. Neither Henry nor Hal actually submits to it, of course. But the prince's final ascendancy, with its cold deflation of Falstaff's most persistent illusion, cannot altogether dispel the atmosphere that prompted his father's disheartening meditation.[8]

No positive alternative to disillusion can be based on the sort of illusion that fosters Shallow's misty memories or Hotspur's "great imagination / Proper to madmen" which "led his powers to death / And winking leaped into destruction" (I, iii, 31–33). The creative energy which Shakespeare sets against dispiriting submission to historical process allies itself with fiction rather than illusion—and with a fiction that is open-eyed to its own relationship with history. *Henry V* stands as a demonstration of the possibilities of such historical fiction. As such, it is not offered as *the* answer that those who despair or err in 2 *Henry IV* have been missing. It does not rule out of play such a devastating speculative glimpse into the book of fate as Henry's or negate the kind of pragmatic analysis of the "time's deceased" that Warwick advocates. 2 *Henry IV* is its own drama and presents its own image of a range of unpromising attitudes toward the past, rather than merely providing a somber stage in Shakespeare's developing ideas about history on their way to their proper "conclusion" in *Henry V*. But *Henry V* offers a viable creative alternative to the bleak or faulty retrospection that prevails in 2 *Henry IV* and reaffirms the potential value of the remembered lost leader in terms that are accountable to the complex questions about the present's relationship to the past that recur through *King John* and the second tetralogy.

CHAPTER EIGHT

Henry V

"Remember with Advantages"

In the second scene of *Henry V*, having evidently satisfied Henry's insistence that his claim to France be made "with right and conscience," the archbishop of Canterbury pulls all the stops to inspire his new king with the fullest possible sense of his heroic heritage:

> Gracious lord,
> Stand for your own, unwind your bloody flag,
> Look back into your mighty ancestors;
> Go, my dread lord, to your great-grandsire's tomb,
> From whom you claim; invoke his warlike spirit,
> And your great-uncle's, Edward the Black Prince,
> Who on the French ground played a tragedy,

Making defeat on the full power of France,
Whiles his most mighty father on a hill
Stood smiling to behold his lion's whelp
Forage in blood of French nobility.
O noble English, that could entertain
With half their forces the full pride of France
And let another half stand laughing by,
All out of work and cold for action!

And the other lords in attendance, both spiritual and temporal, take up the stirring theme:

Ely: Awake remembrance of these valiant dead,
And with your puissant arm renew their feats.
You are their heir; you sit upon their throne;
The blood and courage that renownèd them
Runs in your veins; and my thrice-puissant liege
Is in the very May-morn of his youth,
Ripe for exploits and mighty enterprises.
Exeter: Your brother kings and monarchs of the earth
Do all expect that you should rouse yourself
As did the former lions of your blood.

(100–124)

We have encountered nothing quite like this energetic invocation of heroic exemplars in the entire course of the histories. Note that the thrust here is entirely positive, with none of the chiding (*3HVI*, II, ii, 34 ff.; *RII*, II, i, 171 ff.) or accusation (*3HVI*, II, vi, 14 ff.) or grievance (*2HVI*, I, i, 76 ff.) or regret (*RII*, II, iii, 99 ff.) with which noble counsellors in earlier plays recall lost leaders as they address their lapsed descendants. Rather than the invidious comparison between then and now, old and new, we find here an absolute identification of the present with the past, whose heroes are not lost but will live again through their "ripe" young heir: "*Awake* remembrance" and "*renew* their feats."[1]

Here, then, the ideal of emulation, which had been ignored, violated, or distorted through seven plays since Talbot fulfilled it by "renewing" the dead Salisbury's spirit in his own, is affirmed as never before. The identification of Henry with the "native mightiness" of his "victorious stock," and particularly with the Black Prince, is echoed by the only French leader with enough sense to fear him:

> Think we King Harry strong;
> And, princes, look you strongly arm to meet him.
> The kindred of him hath been fleshed upon us;
> And he is bred out of that bloody strain
> That haunted us in our familiar paths.
> Witness our too much memorable shame
> When Crécy battle fatally was struck,
> And all our princes captived, by the hand
> Of that black name, Edward, Black Prince of Wales;
> Whiles that his mountain sire—on mountain standing,
> Up in the air, crowned with the golden sun—
> Saw his heroical seed, and smiled to see him
> Mangle the work of nature, and deface
> The patterns that by God and by French fathers
> Had twenty years been made. This is a stem
> Of that victorious stock; and let us fear
> The native mightiness and fate of him.
>
> (II, iv, 48–64)

And it is echoed again after Agincourt in the memorable accent of Henry's fellow Welshman, Fluellen:

> Your grandfather of famous memory, . . . and your great-uncle Edward the Plack Prince of Wales, as I have read in the chronicles, fought a most prave pattle here in France.
> (IV, vii, 87–90)

This repeated affirmation of "native mightiness" reborn is bolstered by other features of the play that elevate Henry and his happy few to full heroic stature. Salisbury, who ranked next to Henry himself as a prototype of the fallen exemplar in *1 Henry VI*, puts in a cameo appearance here before Agincourt to cheer his comrades and be cheered in turn (IV, iii, 4–14). The only two English nobles to die on this day of glory are given a battlefield eulogy that recalls such a consummation of soldierly love in mutual heroic death as that of the two Talbots (IV, vi). And classical models join ranks with English ancestors in the praise bestowed on Henry, whether it be by the Chorus ("their conqu'ring Caesar" [V, Chorus, 28]), by the French ("You shall find his vanities forespent / Were but the outside of the Roman Brutus, / Covering discretion with a coat of folly" [II, iv, 36–38]), or by Fluellen ("As Alexander, . . . so also Harry Monmouth" [IV, vii, 11–48]). Henry likewise elevates his own appeal to "native mightiness":

> On, on, you noble English,
> Whose blood is fet from fathers of war-proof,
> Fathers that like so many Alexanders
> Have in these parts from morn till even fought
> And sheathed their swords for lack of argument.
>
> (III, i, 17–21)

The contrast with the previous play, where such lofty allusions were either weighted down with obvious irony or given over to Falstaff and his entourage, is striking. Here they are reserved almost exclusively for references to the king and for the use of that other Welshman well "literatured in the wars." Poor Pistol has to bombast out his empty verse as best he can mostly by other means.

Whether this identification of Henry with (and elevation of him by means of) his heroic forebears, and the consequent affirmation of the past's renewed vitality in the present, is ultimately validated or ironically subverted must depend, of course, on the play's full portrait of the king and his actions. And that central issue of heroic celebration versus ironic subversion in this play has been argued strenuously enough and long enough to have stretched into a Hundred Years War of its own. It would be foolhardy to pretend to resolve the argument here and stifling to review it in detail. To maintain my balance in it, however, I will try to show how various factors emphasized by the ironists do complicate the celebrative portrait in ways that acknowledge the kinds of questions raised about heroical history in the plays that precede *Henry V*. And I will also try to show how such complications allow a celebration of the dead hero and his living potential that gives the "true" past, as represented here, more viability for a reflective present than a simpler exemplary play could hope to offer. Again, rather than reviewing all the pros and cons of Henry's performance, I will focus on those features of it that emphasize the play's understanding of historical perspectives and of the remembered hero's place in them in particular.[2]

The apocryphal *Edward III*, with its direct presentation of Henry's native model, the Black Prince, and of those exploits that are remembered so frequently in Henry's own play, provides an especially useful point of comparison here.[3] There are no such recollections of heroic precedents in *Edward III*, so its presentation of the past is not deepened even in this simple way. Prince Edward is shown as a model for emulation, but since he does not look back at other models, we do not see exemplary history at work *in* the play and thereby becoming a subject *of* the play, as it is in *Henry V* (and already was in *1 Henry VI*). In his final speech, however, the Black Prince does look ahead and in doing so shows the extent of his (and the play's) self-consciousness about his exemplary function for "hereafter ages":

> Now, father, this petition Edward makes
> To thee, whose grace hath bin his strongest shield,
> That, as thy pleasure chose me for the man
> To be the instrument to shew thy power,
> So thou wilt grant that many princes more,
> Bred and brought up within that little Isle,

May still be famous for lyke victories!
And, for my part, the bloudie scars I beare,
The wearie nights that I have watcht in field,
The dangerous conflicts I have often had,
The fearfull menaces were proffered me,
The heate and cold and what else might displease:
I wish were now redoubled twentie fold,
So that hereafter ages, when they reade
The painfull traffike of my tender youth,
Might thereby be inflamd with such resolve,
As not the territories of France alone,
But likewise Spain, Turkie, and what countries els
That iustly would provoke faire England's ire,
Might, at their presence, tremble and retire.

After the accomplishment of Crécy, and with a pious attribution of all credit to God that may remind us of his grand-nephew, Prince Edward presents himself and what he has done for our inspiration. He might wish his hardships were redoubled twenty-fold so that future readers would be all the more inflamed by them, but he has done what he has done, and we see (or can read) that painful traffic for what it so patently (and gloriously) is. He has no sense of actually shaping what he does to advantage (he simply wishes it were more), nor does he conceive of his story being shaped for its readers (or viewers) by the recorder's hand. This play's ideal hero offers himself for our edification as he presumably truly was, and no questions are expected to be asked.

Since the Chorus serves in a much more elaborate way as the presenter of *Henry V*, Henry himself is given no such purposively mediating speech as this one in which the Black Prince presents himself and his play for our admiration. But when Henry does look ahead to his "story" as it will be remembered in the future, he does so with the consciousness that it may be shaped both in the making and in the remembering (or telling)—a consciousness that we might expect of the matured Hal and one that approximates the fuller historical perspective of the play itself:

> If we are marked to die, we are enow
> To do our country loss; and if to live,
> The fewer men, the greater share of honor.
>
> .   .   .   .
>
> This day is called the Feast of Crispian.
> He that outlives this day, and comes safe home,
> Will stand a-tiptoe when this day is namèd
> And rouse him at the name of Crispian.
>
> .   .   .   .
>
> Old men forget; yet all shall be forgot,
> But he'll remember, with advantages,
> What feats he did that day. Then shall our names,
> Familiar in his mouth as household words—
> Harry the King, Bedford and Exeter,
> Warwick and Talbot, Salisbury and Gloucester—
> Be in their flowing cups freshly rememb'red.
> This story shall the good man teach his son;
> And Crispin Crispian shall ne'er go by,
> From this day to the ending of the world,
> But we in it shall be rememberèd—
> We few, we happy few, we band of brothers.
>
> (IV, iii, 20–60)

Part of what gives this speech its effective resonance is that Henry does not step *out* of his time frame, as represented, to address us in ours as audience in the way that the Black Prince does in the summary-choral speech cited above. We see Henry *in* his moment of action anticipating the recreation of that moment, so that we experience something like the same *frisson* of that connection across time that reverberates for us through Cassius's anticipation ("How many ages hence / Shall this our lofty scene be acted over") without the ironic chill that distinguishes our view from the one that Cassius imagines for us ("So often shall the knot of us be called / The men that gave their country liberty" [*JC*, III, i, 111–118]). Henry, rather, foresees the celebration of his memory in precisely the spirit that we are to experience it at this moment in the play. But in doing so, Henry shows (and stimulates in us) the awareness that his "story" can be enhanced both in the doing and the telling. As for the doing, "the fewer men, the greater share of honor." And as for the telling, Henry sanctions in anticipation the very sort of remembering "with advantages," including the "familiar" name dropping, that Falstaff had mocked and we had discredited in the previous play when Shallow had indulged in it. Shallow's self-indulgence was unconscious, of course. Henry's consciousness of this process aligns him with the play's acknowledgment that it may remember this king and his deeds "with advantages" and with its endorsement of such remembrance when it is consciously (and hence responsibly) invoked.[4]

Certainly, this larger sense of the shaping of history both in the making and in the telling adds to Henry's stature as the hero king celebrated in the play. That he sees so much of what the play shows in this regard elevates him in the play's estimation. He incorporates various perspectives on history that have been developed through preceding plays, balancing his understanding of the fictions of history and their uses with a pragmatic analysis of such facts as history affords him as an aid to his foresight (in the manner of 2 *Henry IV*'s Warwick, or of Pandulph):

> We must not only arm t'invade the French,
> But lay down our proportions to defend
> Against the Scot, who will make road upon us
> With all advantages.
>
> .   .   .   .   .
>
> For you shall read that my great-grandfather
> Never went with his forces into France

But that the Scot on his unfurnished kingdom
Came pouring like the tide into a breach.
                    (I, ii, 136–149)

Such informed circumspection validates, in Henry's first appearance, the praise already given his political acumen by the archbishop of Canterbury (I, i, 41–47). This young lion (I, ii, 124)
has the shrewdness of a fox.

But the familiar combination of lion and fox has evolved, for
critical readers, toward the more baffling complex of Rabkin's (or
Gombrich's) rabbit and duck.[5] And it is, of course, the very issue
of Henry's political shrewdness, and of the degree to which his
posture as a model hero king is a "fiction" of self-serving policy,
that divides those readers who see one or the other of these simpler figures in his lineaments—readers who attack Henry (and
interpret the play ironically), on the one hand, or defend him
(and accept the Chorus's celebration of him), on the other. Does
Henry share his father's political motive for the French war,
cynically accept the archbishop's effectual bribe to pursue that
war, and thereby squelch the bill that would relieve the commonwealth at the expense of the wealthy Church? Or does he sin-
cerely "believe in heart" that he ought with "right and conscience
make this claim" according to the archbishop's public argument
(I, ii, 30, 96)? Is he as humbly pious as he seems, or does he give
all credit for his achievements to God (and lay all responsibility
for his actions on other shoulders) in order to promote his own
image and serve his political interest? Readers and audiences may
answer these questions (or the latter may have them answered by
directors and actors), but the play does not. By contrast with both
parts of *Henry IV*, where we were given a privileged view of Hal
in his first scenes and learned there his private thoughts about his
public role before he ever appeared in it, *Henry V* gives us the
king in his public role first and foremost. With one exception
(which does not directly answer—or even address—the questions

asked above), we see no more of him than might be seen "histori-cally" by others who could make report of him. We may speculate with these others (Ely and Canterbury in I, i, or Bedford, Exeter, and Westmoreland at the opening of II, ii) or be guided by their speculations, but in this play we have little interpretive advantage over them in such matters. In this regard, as in so many others, Henry is the opposite of the only other Shakespearean king to so dominate the play named for him. The villain, Richard, confided in us from the beginning, but we see only the "performance" of the hero, Henry, and must understand it as best we can without the help of "backstage" preparations or reflections.

The one sequence in which we do see and hear Henry alone scarcely clarifies matters for us. His first soliloquy, following his encounter with the three soldiers who refuse to show "the mettle of . . . [their] pasture" quite so gratifyingly as he might hope "good yeomen" should when he prompts them into a discussion of the king, is not a confidential exposition in Richard's manner (or in Hal's of *1 Henry IV*, I, ii) but a meditation that strays from the issues just joined about the merits of the king's cause in France and its consequences for his followers (IV, i; III, i, 25–27). As he deflates the only distinctive gift bestowed on kings, the "idol Ceremony," he shows a complex consciousness that sets him apart from such single-minded heroes as Talbot or Richmond or Hotspur, and his envy of the wretched slave's "vacant mind" im-plies its opposite in the restive thoughts that fill his own sleepless royal head. But, again by contrast with Richard, what plans or motives might be included in those private night thoughts, or how his present course of action might be reckoned (or recon-ciled) in the nocturnal "watch the king keeps to maintain the peace," we know not, although the prayer he then addresses to the "God of battles" (his only other soliloquy in the play) surely reveals one nagging thorn in the insomniac's "bed majestical." It is noteworthy that instead of invoking the "warlike spirit" of his great uncle, the Black Prince, or any other such happy precedent, at this crucial juncture Henry recalls his father's fault "in compassing the crown," for which he knows his expensive efforts at atonement cannot actually avail (IV, i, 275–292). Even in prayer, it is not altogether clear whether Henry's piety is primary in itself or primarily pragmatic. But either way, we see here his full awareness that he is *in* history and must face its consequences—that, for all his clear purpose to shape it, he cannot simply *make* history (or his story) according to his will, as Richard Gloucester sets out to do.[6]

The presentation of Henry himself then, both public and (to the limited extent that we get it at all) private, offers us a complex image that will not fit neatly into the simple pattern of the exemplary hero whose spirit he is urged to renew. If that complexity emerges partly through his own alert sense of history and its uses, of the means by which his "place i' th' story" can and cannot be effectively shaped to advantage, and if that awareness better equips him for his role than any other leader in these plays, it is nonetheless true that we are allowed to question him in ways that simply are not made relevant to the presentation of other "model" heroes. Such questions must be pushed more aggressively and single-mindedly than the play itself encourages us to do in order to subvert the portrait into straight irony, surely, but ignoring them also amounts to willful distortion of a play that begins by showing us how Henry's French war will serve the interests of the Church at the expense of the commonwealth. It is as though Shakespeare is determined to present "Harry like himself" in the sense that he will not omit details that give the king "such a questionable shape," at the same time that he refuses to offer us necessarily fictive access to Henry's private plans and motives which would give more answers to such questions "than history can pattern." He thus abides to this extent by the given limits of historical truth here and acknowledges in this sense (different from the Chorus's) that the entire Harry "like himself" cannot be shown (or even known).

This complex image, which modifies pure celebration without turning into its ironic opposite, is reinforced by other elements in the play that awake remembrance of the dead (valiant and otherwise) and thereby reflect on the past's effective value in the present and on the possible realization of that value through Henry. The play's most insistent advocate of exemplary history is, of course, Captain Fluellen. The Welshman does not merely invoke heroic models and cite instructive precedents on a given occasion, as others may do. He is an enthusiast who would meet *every* modern instance with an ancient prescription. For Fluellen, the past not only lives in the present as a vital source of inspiration and instruction; it should dominate the present absolutely, ruling all actions according to the letter as well as the spirit. Thus we first meet him excoriating his Irish colleague, Captain Macmorris, for directing the duke of Gloucester to use mines at the siege of Harfleur because "the mines is not according to the disciplines of the war" (III, ii, 53–54); and for Fluellen, though he has "read in chronicles" about the "prave pattle" the Black Prince fought at Crécy (IV, vii, 87–90), to be well "literatured in the wars" (142) is to be "of great expedition and knowledge in th' aunchient wars" (III, ii, 71–72), not to have studied in some modern school of mines. "The true disciplines of the wars" is, "look you, . . . the Roman disciplines, . . . the disciplines of the pristine wars of the Romans" (66–74).

A distinction might be made, of course, between such instructive study of "discipline" in the conduct of war and the invocation of heroic precedents. Whereas the latter calls up noble virtues for inspiration, the former might seem a pragmatic and analytical use of classical military history for purposes akin to Machiavelli's political "discourses" on Roman history. So, in Fluellen's terms, the invidious comparison between Pompey's strict camp and the laxness of the English on the eve of Agincourt is meant to be instructive rather than inspirational:

> If you would take the pains but to examine the wars of
> Pompey the Great, you shall find, I warrant you, that there
> is no tiddle taddle nor pibble pabble in Pompey's camp. I

warrant you, you shall find the ceremonies of the wars, and
the cares of it, and the forms of it, and the sobriety of it,
and the modesty of it, to be otherwise. (IV, i, 68–73)

But for Fluellen no such distinction between useful examples and
heroic exemplars really exists. His ancients are all, like Pompey,
paragons, and "excellent discipline" merges readily with high
moral virtues when he graces a present action with ancient labels:

> The Duke of Exeter is as magnanimous as Agamemnon,
> and a man that I love and honor with my soul, and my
> heart, and my duty, and my live, and my living, and my
> uttermost power. He is not—God be praised and plessed!—
> any hurt in the orld, but keeps the pridge most valiantly,
> with excellent discipline. There is an aunchient lieutenant
> there at the pridge, I think in my very conscience he is as
> valiant a man as Mark Anthony, and he is a man of no esti-
> mation in the orld, but I did see him do as gallant service.
> (III, vi, 6–15)

And, of course, it is just this failure to make distinctions and
discriminations, aggravated by his comical verbal lapses, that
renders Fluellen's account of the world according to ancient precedent so palpably inadequate. We later learn that for Fluellen
"the pig, or the great, or the mighty, or the huge, or the magnanimous are all one reckonings, save the phrase is a little variations" (IV, vii, 14–17), and by such imprecise "reckonings" great
Agamemnon may be "magnanimous," though it would scarcely
be the epithet for him that would leap to most minds. A very little
more experience will cure Fluellen of his delusion that Pistol is a
Mark Antony, but his simple faith that all things ancient are the
proper measures of all things modern is as incurable as it is
inflexible.

The simplicity that shines through Fluellen's gratification in his
tautological explication of Fortune's emblems (III, vi, 29–37),
the inflexibility that leads him to weigh the thieving Bardolph

("For if, look you, he were my prother, I would desire the duke to use his good pleasure and put him to execution; for discipline ought to be used" [III, vi, 53–55]) equally with the stalwart Williams ("An please your majesty, let his neck answer for it, if there is any martial law in the orld" [IV, viii, 39–40]), and the obliviousness to distinctions that naturally accompanies inflexible simplicity ("But 'tis all one; 'tis alike as my fingers is to my fingers" [IV, vii, 27–28]) are nowhere more evident than in his strenuous forcing of Henry himself into grooves reluctantly supplied by the ancient model of "Alexander the Pig" (11–48). The result is caricature, of course—striking enough caricature, as he piles one fatuous similitude on another to build his case ("There is a river in Macedon, and there is also moreover a river at Monmouth"), to prompt Richard Levin's nomination of Fluellen as the eponymous patron of all critics who force thematic readings into place by similar means.[7] The question here is what effect the caricature has on our view of Henry, who is the immediate object of Fluellen's praise, and on the whole method of exemplary history with which Fluellen bulldozes his single-minded way through the play. And the answer should not be as one-dimensional as Fluellen's answers always are. Obviously, both the monarch and the method are rendered subject here to ironies of a sort that never ripple the simpler surface of an instructive and celebratory play such as *Edward III*. By giving this intrepid advocate of exemplary history so conspicuous a role in his own historical play, Shakespeare alerts us to (and signals the play's awareness of) the shortcomings of any view of the past and its relationship to the present so radically oversimplified that it is "out of doubt, and out of question too, and ambiguities" (V, i, 40–41).[8]

That its hero can be praised by association with "the Pig" is only one of the doubts, questions, and ambiguities that this play allows to cluster around Henry and to modify any easy elevation of the English to a purely heroic plane by likening them to "so many Alexanders" (III, i, 19). Unlike the strictly exemplary mode and use of history cited and favored by Fluellen, *Henry V* does include such tiddle taddle and pibble pabble as Fluellen's own extravagant analogy between Monmouth and Macedon and their favorite sons, not to mention the even more extravagant vein of Pistol and his cohorts. This *inclusiveness* both lends authenticity to the historical portrait and prompts questions about Henry, just as the *inconclusiveness* about Henry's own private thoughts and motives does.

But if Fluellen's presence helps to distinguish this play from the purely didactic history (and its war from "the pristine wars of the Romans") to which he himself is so wholly devoted, the play's view of Fluellen does not simply subvert him or his stance. He may miss the mark occasionally, and he can never see (through his single lens) the fuller perspective we are afforded, but he is seldom altogether wrong and never spurned or rejected by any consciousness more elevated than Pistol's—certainly not by the larger consciousness that the play grants to its implied audience. If he and his way of thinking come short, they mean well. As he insists in his honest but tactless offer of money to the ruffled Williams, "it is with a good will" that he confronts a world more complex than he is (IV, viii, 63). And by regarding him with more tolerance than his own rigid posture could ever muster, the play gives its qualified blessing to the simplistic understanding of history-as-lesson-book that he embodies and it so far surpasses. As for Henry, it is not for the limited likes of Fluellen to pass the play's ultimate judgment on him, even unconsciously, by comparing him to "the Pig" (consciously, of course, Fluellen grants Henry the supreme honor of being his Welsh countryman: "I need not be ashamed of your majesty, praised be God, so long as your majesty is an honest man" [IV, vii, 107–109]). Rather the reverse, and we are bound to assent to Henry's own qualified but positive assessment of Fluellen: "Though it appear a little out of fashion, / There is much care and valor in this Welshman" (IV, i, 81–82). Here, where it shows plainly for a moment (the two lines are a "soliloquette"), Henry's consciousness is at one with the play's, and we may safely extend the qualified commendation of Fluellen's care and valor to his unflagging and uncomplicated devotion to the lessons of the "valiant dead."

Fluellen's attitude, however well meaning, is nowhere less adequate than in his assessment of Henry's rejection of the Welsh captain's absolute opposite, "the fat knight with the great pelly doublet" (IV, vii, 40–46). In its treatment of Falstaff, the play gives a remarkable twist to its "remembrance of these valiant dead" and to the history plays' recurrent figure of the lost leader. Surprisingly, Falstaff himself here fills the role allotted in earlier plays to the dead hero whose loss makes such a difference to the bereaved and diminished present: the role (however varied) of Henry himself in *1 Henry VI*, of Talbot in its sequels, of Richard Cordelion in *John*, of the Black Prince in *Richard II*, and of Hotspur in *2 Henry IV*. And, in his accustomed "manner of wrenching the true cause the false way" (*2HIV*, II, i, 105–106), the dead Falstaff prompts us to think of the role he assumes here in inverted terms: the dead antihero, or the unvaliant dead, or the lost misleader.

Such terms, however, and the inversion they express share the absolute simplicity of Fluellen's view, which they suggest fairly enough. The negation of Falstaff is the particular point of praise toward which Fluellen's long comparison of Henry with "Alexander the Pig" labors:

> As Alexander killed his friend Cleitus, being in his ales and
> his cups, so also Harry Monmouth, being in his right wits
> and his good judgments, turned away the fat knight with
> the great pelly doublet. He was full of jests, and gipes,
> and knaveries, and mocks. I have forgot his name. (IV, vii,
> 40–46)

As is most often the case, Fluellen is wrongly simple rather than simply wrong. It is, quite evidently, to Henry's acknowledged credit as hero king that he turned away Falstaff and turned away from all that Falstaff represents in the public view so carefully nurtured by Hal through the two preceding plays. As we have noted, that public view is the first and primary one we are offered of Henry in this play, and Canterbury states its glowing response to the king's rejection of "the courses of his youth" in the first scene. Whether from such a perspective or according to the absolute rule of "disciplines" that guides Fluellen, turning away Falstaff was as clearly right as the king's endorsement of Bardolph's execution for robbing a French church.

But here, more intensively than anywhere else in the play, we are given a private view that directly counters the "orthodox" version. And here, as nowhere else, the king's own consciousness, for all we can know, is as limited as Fluellen's. As though to enforce a simple inversion of the role of the dead hero who lives in remembrance to inspire the present, Fluellen has forgotten Falstaff's name. And Henry, "that ever-living man of memory" (*1HVI*, IV, iii, 51), shows no more recollection of Falstaff than he does (despite Fluellen's explicit prompting) of Bardolph when he approves the latter's execution (III, vi, 98–104). We can only speculate whether or not his forgetfulness here is as studied as it clearly was in the preceding play's rejection scene ("I know thee not, old man"), but either way its effect is to distance Henry from us. Whereas in other respects—and particularly in his evident awareness of the nature and uses of history—Henry's consciousness approximates the play's own in its scope by contrast with Fluellen's rigidly limited view, in this one important instance he shows (whatever he may think) no larger vision than his fellow Welshman. He is therefore vulnerable in his "forgetfulness" to all the doubts and questions and ambiguities that the play awakens through its sympathetic remembrance of the not-so-valiant dead knight. And no lost leader is remembered with more poignant regret or colors our view of the present action more vividly than Falstaff.[9]

That remembrance occupies two scenes of the second act, which as a whole provides an interim between the eager resolve of Act One ("Therefore, my lords, omit no happy hour / That may give furth'rance to our expedition; / For we have now no thought in us but France" [ii, 301–303]) and the actual commencement of the "fair action" in Act Three ("Once more unto the breach, dear friends" [i, 1]). It is as though the play's (and the king's) forward thrust is suspended unexpectedly for this lingering reminiscence of the "forgotten" companion—an effect that is emphasized by the odd doubling back of the final choral couplet introducing Act Two and again by the evident simultaneity of Henry's triumphant departure and Falstaff's troubled demise.[10] "'A parted ev'n just between twelve and one, ev'n at the turning o' th' tide" (II, iii, 12–13), we hear the hostess (ever a stickler for detail) report in the quiet hush just after the flourish with which the king sets sail: "Cheerly to sea the signs of war advance" (II, ii, 192). As the king catches his swelling tide, we are made to feel the ebbing of Falstaff's with a sentiment that perhaps no one but the hostess—for whom "a good heart's worth gold" (*2HIV*, II, iv, 29–30)—could unleash so feelingly. If we, like the archbishop of Canterbury, admire the king in his chosen spheres "of commonwealth affairs, . . . of war, . . . [and] of policy" (I, i, 40–45) for the mastery of discourse that sets him so far above honest Fluellen, in this "forgotten" sphere it is left for the hostess with her malapropisms, Pistol with his rodomontade, and the normally inarticulate Nym ("I cannot tell") with his skimpy supply of verbal crutches to pay tribute to the one character who could ever match words with the younger Henry. And they do it superbly. Note the insistence on sentiment that might seem mawkish in more sophisticated mouths:

> *Hostess*: By my troth, he'll yield the crow a pudding one of these days. The king has killed his heart. . . . Ah, poor heart! he is so shaked of a burning quotidian tertian that it is most lamentable to behold. Sweet men, come to him.

Nym: The king hath run bad humors on the knight; that's the even of it.

Pistol: Nym, thou hast spoke the right. His heart is fracted and corroborate.

(II, i, 83–120)

The emphasis on human feeling and suffering through the repeated references to the old knight's broken heart—and to him *as* "poor heart" (it was his last plaintive word to Hal become Henry: "My king! My Jove! I speak to thee, my heart!" [*2HIV*, V, v, 47])—is one measure of the distance between the companionable world Henry has banished and the heroic one in which he now sets his course. "Heart" is essential there, too, but as an organ of courage (in the tradition of Coeur-de-lion), not of love: "O England! model to thy inward greatness, / Like little body with a mighty heart" (II, Chorus, 16–17). Back in Eastcheap, even manly Pistol acknowledges those softer places in the heart that the blast of war is supposed to stiffen:

Hostess: Prithee, honey-sweet husband, let me bring thee to Staines.

Pistol: No; for my manly heart doth earn.

Bardolph, be blithe; Nym, rouse thy vaunting veins;

Boy, bristle thy courage up; for Falstaff he is dead,

And we must earn therefore.

(II, iii, 1–6)

By the benevolence of the hostess's illiteracy, Falstaff is consigned to the eternal custody of England's primal lost leader: "He's in Arthur's bosom, if ever man went to Arthur's bosom" (9–10). And no one can manage better than poor Nym to balance the play's celebration of its hero king with the fuller truth about him that Falstaff's death and lingering memory impress upon us: "The king is a good king, but it must be as it may: he passes some humors and careers" (II, i, 121–122).

Falstaff serves here, then, as a characteristically unique permu-ation of the lost leader figure—a dead antihero whom the living hero must *forget* in order to fulfill his own role as leader but whose remembrance colors our view of that hero and reminds us of what he has lost in his triumph. Falstaff's is not, however, the ultimate appearance of the lost leader figure in the histories. That distinction belongs to Henry himself, whom we thus see in double perspective in this final play of the series. Within the play proper, where we see him "in the very May-morn of his youth" (I, ii, 120), the living Henry awakens remembrance of those valiant dead who preceded him and renews their feats with his puissant arm. But from the vantage point of the Chorus, who shares *our* time-frame and presents the play to us, Henry himself is the valiant dead hero whose remembrance the play awakens. And it is the Chorus who actively guides our awareness that we are watching a historical fiction, with full emphasis on both the history *and* the fiction, so that we see the staged renewal of Henry and his feats "perspectively" (to borrow the French king's term [V, ii, 307]).[11]

Here, then, is an answer to Samuel Johnson's sensible query about the presence of a Chorus in this particular play: "Nor can it be easily discovered why the intelligence given by the Chorus is more necessary in this play than in many others where it is omitted."[12] It is particularly to the point of this history play to keep us in mind of the relationship between the presentation we watch and the "true things" it professes to imitate or represent (IV, Chorus, 53). And our awareness of that relationship involves more, of course, than the reminder that "the stage is only a stage."[13] As directed by the Chorus, we address the possibility of realizing the positive force of the past in the present.

From the very beginning, even before he turns to the inevitable inadequacies of "this unworthy scaffold to bring forth / So great an object," the Chorus appeals to the capacity of "invention" which he consistently acknowledges as the basis of any recreated history. Prior to the difficulty of visibly representing "the vasty fields of France" and all that happened thereon is the question of apprehending what *did* happen thereon. Prior to the performance of the play is the construction of the story, and from first to last the Chorus reminds us that the story is not simply *there* (or not *simply* there) but has to be found ("pursued") and composed by the struggling author in order to be presented: "Thus far, with rough and all-unable pen, / Our bending author hath pursued the story" (Epilogue, 1–2). The insistence on composition, on "authoring," incorporates the awareness that history is not merely recorded and reported fact in the raw, that the past is conceived, construed, and shaped by those who "remember" and tell its story. This is the process of recreation that we have seen dramatized more and more openly from the hopeful duke of York in *1 Henry VI* through the regretful duke of York in *Richard II* to the wistful Shallow in *2 Henry IV*. The Chorus articulates what we have inferred from those earlier plays, and especially from *King John* and the second tetralogy: that history, as men conceive and use it, is also fiction, reconstructed according to the more or less capable lights of those who tell its story. Thus, in the absence of direct access to the past itself and in the presence of a necessarily imperfect mockery of it, we are openly invited to participate in a reconstructive effort that depends on invention, on imagination: "And let us, ciphers to this great accompt, / On your imaginary forces work. / Suppose . . ." (Prologue, 17–19).[14]

But at the same time, the Chorus insists on an *actual* history toward which imagination reaches and of which both the author's story and the actors' play are "all-unable" reproductions. Acknowledgment of the inevitable and necessary fictions of history does not erase all distinctions between fiction and history or mean that history is conceived in terms of pure invention or imagination. The actual Harry may not be accessible to our view exactly "like himself," but an actual Harry is posited. If the presented story must be the work of invention and imagination, those faculties aim at the reality that lies behind and beyond any presentation rather than being set free to conceive the king in whatever shape (rabbit or duck) might best suit the beholder. Thus we are asked to mind "*true* things by what their mock'ries be" (IV, Chorus, 53; emphasis added). Awareness that "men may construe things after their fashion, / Clean from the purpose of the things themselves" (*Julius Caesar*, I, iii, 34–35) does not license us here to indulge in the pleasant vagaries of a Shallow or to be driven headlong by imagination Hotspurlike but obliges us to construe the "things themselves" as truly as we can.

There are, then, two conceptual dimensions beyond that of the "mock'ries" we watch in the presented action. One is the fuller "story" of Henry that has been recorded (and thus composed), to which the Chorus alludes and on which he can draw in the narrative portions of his interims:

> Vouchsafe to those that have not read the story
> That I may prompt them; and of such as have,
> I humbly pray them to admit th'excuse
> Of time, of numbers, and due course of things
> Which cannot in their huge and proper life
> Be here presented.
>
> (V, Chorus, 1–6)

And beyond that story is the full truth, the "huge and proper life" itself, that any account can only approximate. All three dimensions may be incorporated in the term "history" as the Chorus uses it in the Prologue:

> Admit me Chorus to this history,
> Who, Prologue-like, your humble patience pray,
> Gently to hear, kindly to judge, our play.
>
> (32–34)

"This history" can be "our play," or the dramatized version of Henry's story, for which the Chorus serves as presenter. But the Chorus also mediates between the fuller story (or history) and the play with its abridgments, "jumping o'er times" (29). And he also reminds us of the actual "accomplishment of many years"

(30) that are the entire past, or history itself, of which any written or presented version must be an imperfect record. We are asked, with the aid of the ciphers onstage and the Chorus's verbal prompting, to imagine the reality (if not *all* the scopic and temporal detail—our thoughts, too, must jump over times) of this ultimate dimension.

When the chorus does prompt us to imagine in our mind's ear and eye the actual events behind the acted performance, one primary effect is to collapse the time that separates us from these past events. Instead of sharing our current retrospect, as he does when he speaks of the performance, he takes us with him to the moment of the action itself:

> *Now* all the youth of England are on fire,
> And silken dalliance in the wardrobe lies.
> *Now* thrive the armorers, and honor's thought
> Reigns solely in the breast of every man.
> $\qquad\qquad$ (II, 1–4; emphasis added)

The openly intended effect is to place us *there* in thought and feeling, so that our breasts too stir with the excitement and expectation of the moment—so that we "see" and "hear" the very sights and sounds of Henry's expedition:

> Play with your fancies, and in them behold
> Upon the hempen tackle shipboys climbing;
> Hear the shrill whistle which doth order give
> To sounds confused; behold the threaden sails,
> Borne with th'invisible and creeping wind,
> Draw the huge bottoms through the furrowed sea,
> Breasting the lofty surge. O, do but think
> You stand upon the rivage and behold
> A city on th'inconstant billows dancing;
> For so appears this fleet majestical,
> Holding due course to Harfleur. Follow, follow!
> $\qquad\qquad$ (III, 7–17)

Caught up thus, we join the expedition, for "who is he" who would not?

> Grapple your minds to sternage of this navy,
> And leave your England as dead midnight still,
> Guarded with grandsires, babies, and old women,
> Either past or not arrived to pith and puissance;
> For who is he whose chin is but enriched
> With one appearing hair that will not follow
> These culled and choice-drawn cavaliers to France?
>
> (18–24)

Note that it is *our* England in whose eager spirit we share here, and by the same token we are included in the second Chorus's apostrophe *to* England:

> O England! model to thy inward greatness,
> Like little body with a mighty heart,
> What mightst thou do that honor would thee do,
> Were all thy children kind and natural!
>
> (16–19)

The England addressed here is both Henry's, in which France finds out a nest of hollow bosoms, and ours, to which the exhortation speaks with equal force. Having carried us back to Henry's time ("*Now* all the youth of England are on fire"), the Chorus's keenly felt response to the few treacherous conspirators of that time carries forward to our present, and the two times merge in the constant of little England and its mighty heart.

This merging of past and present has clear and strong implications for the living efficacy of the valiant dead, and the Chorus spells out those implications in his penultimate appearance, describing Henry's triumphant return after Agincourt:

> But now behold,
> In the quick forge and working-house of thought,
> How London doth pour out her citizens!

The mayor and all his brethren in best sort,
Like to the senators of th' antique Rome,
With the plebeians swarming at their heels,
Go forth and fetch their conqu'ring Caesar in;
As, by a lower but by loving likelihood,
Were *now* the general of our gracious empress,
As in good time he may, from Ireland coming,
Bringing rebellion broachèd on his sword,
How many would the peaceful city quit
To welcome him! Much more, and much more cause,
Did they this Harry. *Now* in London place him.

(V, 22–35; emphasis added)

As though in fulfillment of young Prince Edward's bright thought, remembering Caesar in the dark shadow of the Tower, that "death makes no conquest of this conqueror, / For now he lives in fame, though not in life" (*RIII*, III, i, 87–88), Caesar lives still in Henry, as Henry can live anew in Essex. Just as Henry renews the feats of his mighty ancestors in the play, so (though by a necessarily lower likelihood, Essex being no king but only "the general of our gracious empress") we may see a live reenactment of Henry's triumph, as the play describes it, in "our" time. The Chorus's reference to the audience's current hopes gives specific shape and body to the faith Lucy expressed over the dead Talbots: "From their ashes shall be reared / A phoenix" (*1HVI*, IV, vii, 92–93). Faith in the continuity linking England's present directly to its heroic past—the faith that seemed shaken in the "new world" of *Richard II* and lost in the old world of *2 Henry IV*—is reaffirmed fully and explicitly by the Chorus, who is, of course, in a position to apply the play's past to the audience's present more fully and explicitly than any character we have yet encountered.[15]

But in the very process of asserting this continuity in such specific terms, the Chorus shifts perspective in a way that modifies the effective realization of the past as present that he just evoked.

Notice how his "now" shifts from "now behold," which puts us at Henry's triumphal return, to "were now the general of our gracious empress . . . coming," which brings us back to our Elizabethan time-frame and moves Henry's welcome home back into retrospect ("Much more . . . / Did they this Harry"), and finally to "now in London place him" (rather than "behold him"), which refers us to the immediate occasion of the performance under way and its movement from scene to scene, "jumping o'er times." Having "placed" Henry in London for this narrated scene, we are then to

> omit
> All the occurrences, whatever chanced,
> Till Harry's back-return again to France.
> There must we bring him; and myself have played
> The interim, by rememb'ring you 'tis past.
> Then brook abridgment; and your eyes advance,
> After your thoughts, straight back again to France.
>
> (39–45)

The application of past to present, which is enforced in part by making us feel the very spirit of the past as though we were actually there, also, as it becomes overt, brings us back to the present and then leads into the open reminder that we are watching (and participating in) a fictive recreation of that past.

The shifts in perspective through which the Chorus guides us here are characteristic of his "interims." The second likewise begins with vivid evocations of that "now" when "all the youth of England" are (or were) on fire to follow Henry and ends with the "now" of the performance through choral scene setting: "There is the playhouse now, there must you sit" (1, 36). And the third, having beguiled us into hearing the shrill whistles and seeing the swelling sails of Henry's departing fleet, brings us back with a bang ("*Alarum, and chambers go off*") to the business of stage presentation: "Still be kind, / And eke out our performance with your mind" (34–35). Just as he coaxes us into the illusion that we apprehend the actual historical event in our imagination, the Chorus reminds us that the staged performance of that event is a fictive representation, and reminds us especially of the inevitable gap between any such representation and the true "history." And though he asserts the positive renewal of the past more directly than even *1 Henry VI* had implied its possibility, this awareness of the gap between recreation and actuality, between the performance and the "truth" it attempts to present, complicates that assertion and our understanding of it in ways that were not a concern of that earlier play.

The Chorus's acknowledgment of the distance between any representation and the full truth might, if generalized, be applied to the flagrant disparities between his verbal descriptions and the action we see onstage: between the expectations of "warlike Harry" raised by the Prologue and the backroom discussion of Canterbury's politic offer to help finance the war in the opening scene; between the second Chorus's stirring assertion that "honor's thought / Reigns solely in the breast of every man" and our subsequent view of the thoughts that stir the likes of Pistol and Nym; between the fourth Chorus's account of "Harry in the night" comforting "every wretch" on Agincourt eve with his "cheerful substance and sweet majesty" and the uncomfortable scene in which the disguised Henry argues the king's case with the skeptical Williams. These discrepancies prompt some readers to see the performance and its relationship to the truth in terms that virtually invert the Chorus's account of it. Whereas the Chorus apologizes for the performance's failure to express the full truth, which he indicates would give us an even more majestic Henry, ironists see the play proper as exposing the full truth about Henry that subverts the Chorus's idealized portrait. Thus Goddard: "Through the Choruses, the playwright gives us the popular idea of his hero. In the play, the poet tells us the truth about him."[16] And, quite apparently, the play proper *does* expose Henry to questions that form no part of the Chorus's celebration—questions that are all the more pointed because of the juxtaposition of the play's more inclusive presentation with the Chorus's heightened praise. One effect of this juxtaposition is to give a validating sense of completeness to the performance's depiction of Henry and his enterprise in France, despite the Chorus's repeated apologies for its skimpy insufficiency. As we have seen, our view of Agincourt includes the sort of tiddle taddle and pibble pabble that pure celebration or the simple exemplary history favored by Fluellen ignores. And as we have seen, that inclusiveness allows the complications and modifications that are adumbrated by Nym's philosophical qualifying clause: "The king is a good king, but it must be as it may."

If, however, the Chorus's more "pristine" portrait of the hero king paradoxically lends fuller credit to the "unworthy" performance for which he apologizes, measuring the play's Henry with reference to the Chorus by no means simply diminishes him. For it is the *play's* Henry who shares the Chorus's awareness of the fictive dimension of history, and the same Henry who, for all his realization of the hard facts of his own heritage, sanctions the value of remembering "with advantages" when a truly heroic occasion is to be celebrated. And that, in effect, is what we see the Chorus doing and what he invites us to do with him. The darker and harder hues of the play set off the Chorus's own remembrance of the valiant dead as a heightened fictive reconstruction. But that it is such—and is openly seen to *be* such—does not subvert it in a play that acknowledges that all historical portraits are necessarily fictive approximations of an inaccessible truth. In the play proper we see not the "whole truth" but one kind of representation of it that includes elements disadvantageous to the king along with elements that show him to advantage. The Chorus, in another mode, "remembers with advantages." The play entire, including both modes, offers both frankly as fictions of history. The full affirmation of the valiant dead and their vital relationship to the

present comes with full awareness that they cannot be appre-
hended completely and that a Fluellenlike purification of them
into exemplary models ought to be recognized and accepted
as such.[17]

But to acknowledge the fictive dimension of history and to
admit that the best and the brightest may shine both best and
brightest when heightened by "advantages" is *not* to abandon all
commitment to the hopeful proposition that "the truth should
live from age to age" or to subvert all faith in the inspirational
value of the past in the present. The one point where Henry's
historical (or at least prophetic) vision clearly fails him works,
paradoxically, to validate the play's celebration of him and his accomplishment. If Henry has shared in anticipation the Chorus's
retrospective view of Agincourt, the two part company altogether
in the play's concluding sequences. Henry spices his superfluous
wooing of Katherine by imagining their heroic offspring-to-be:

> Shall not thou and I, between Saint Denis and Saint
> George, compound a boy, half French, half English, that
> shall go to Constantinople and take the Turk by the beard?
> (V, ii, 200–203)

But the Chorus, as Epilogue, reminds us of the true sequel:

> Henry the Sixth, in infant bands crowned King
>   Of France and England, did this king succeed;
> Whose state so many had the managing
>   That they lost France and made his England bleed.

The effect is deflation back into reality of what might otherwise
seem a heroic romance's conclusion to this history play, and such
a deflation might serve as capstone to an ironic reading of "warlike Harry's" victory in France. But the irony, precisely because it
confirms the play's ultimate commitment to historical truth insofar as it *can* be known, implies its positive counterpart as well.
There may be no conquest of Constantinople in the offing, and

no happier reign to come than that of Henry VI, but by the same true token there *was* an Agincourt and a Henry V who won it. That is no fiction, even if it is a truth that can only be recreated fictively, and the play asks us to celebrate that heroic feat as true, to share in its spirit by awakening its remembrance, and thus to realize in our present the vitalizing potential of this past accomplishment, even though we should recognize with the play that we cannot apprehend the complete historical truth, that any reconstruction of it such as the play presents must only approximate that truth, and that any simple celebration of it such as the Chorus's must cleanse away darker touches and tougher questions that the play in its entirety includes. Given such acknowledgments, the Chorus, as he makes his final apology, also implicitly claims that this play *has* made its lost leader live anew for us:

> Thus far, with rough and all-unable pen,
>   Our bending author hath pursued the story,
> In little room confining mighty men,
>   Mangling by starts the full course of their glory.
> Small time; but in that small most greatly lived
>   This Star of England.

That "small time" refers both to the actual "full course" of historical events (all too short) here partially portayed and to the mangled starts and confined room of the play itself, the two hours' traffic of the stage, in which "most greatly lived" once more "this Star of England." The fiction is not *all*-unable, and by professing its limits it gains all the more credit for the greatness it celebrates as a truth that should live from age to age.[18]

NOTES

Introduction

1. Citations are from *The Complete Pelican Shakespeare*, ed. Alfred Harbage (1969; New York: Viking Press, 1977).

2. Sir John Froissart, *Chronicles of England, France, Spain, Portugal, Scotland, Brittany, Flanders, and the Adjoining Countries*, trans. John Bourchier, Lord Berners, repr. from Pynson's edition of 1523 and 1525 (London, 1812), 1.

3. E. M. W. Tillyard, *Shakespeare's History Plays* (1944; Harmondsworth: Penguin Books, 1962), 55–57.

4. Thomas Nashe, *Pierce Penilesse His Supplication to the Divell*, in *The Works of Thomas Nashe*, ed. Ronald B. McKerrow, 5 vols. (London: Sidgwick and Jackson, 1910), 1: 212. For more substantial reviews of the tradition of heroical history on which Shakespeare drew, see David Riggs, *Shakespeare's Heroical Histories: "Henry VI" and Its Literary Tradition* (Cambridge, Mass.: Harvard University Press, 1971), and David Quint, "'Alexander the Pig': Shakespeare on History and Poetry," *Boundary* 10 (1982): 49–68. Later notes will indicate how my argument relates to those of Riggs and Quint.

5. See F. Smith Fussner, *The Historical Revolution: English Historical Writing and Thought, 1580–1640* (New York: Columbia University Press; London: Routledge and Kegan Paul, 1962), and F. J. Levy, *Tudor Historical Thought* (San Marino: Huntington Library, 1967), for instructive accounts of the topics accurately identified in their titles.

6. Quoted by Hayden White, *Tropics of Discourse: Essays in Cultural Criticism* (Baltimore: Johns Hopkins University Press, 1978), 36.

7. See ibid. and the introduction to Hayden White, *Metahistory: The Historical Imagination in Nineteenth-Century Europe* (Baltimore: Johns Hopkins University Press, 1973).

8. See, for example, Herbert Lindenberger, *Historical Drama: The Relation of Literature and Reality* (Chicago: University of Chicago Press, 1975), and David Scott Kastan, "'To Set a Form upon that Indigest': Shakespeare's Fictions of History," *CompD* 17 (1983): 1–16. I would also like to give special acknowledgment to the presentations of Professors Lindenberger and Kastan, along with those of Gabriele Bernhard Jackson, F. J. Levy, Bernard McElroy, Phyllis Rackin, and other participants at the 1986 Ohio Shakespeare Conference, *Fact into Fiction: Shakespeare and the Uses of History in the Renaissance*, which I had the pleasure of chairing at Ohio State University. My "Truth in *King John*," *SEL* 23 (1985): 397–417, also addresses this topic.

9. This is my feeling about the sophisticated metadramatic reading presented by John W. Blanpied, *Time and the Artist in Shakespeare's English Histories* (Newark: University of Delaware Press, 1983).

10. Robert Ornstein, *A Kingdom for a Stage: The Achievement of Shakespeare's History Plays* (Cambridge, Mass.: Harvard University Press, 1972). Credit must also be given here to A. P. Rossiter's "Ambivalence: The Dialectic of the Histories," repr. in his *Angel with Horns and Other Shakespearean Lectures*, ed. Graham Storey (London: Longmans, Green, 1961), 40–64. Henry Ansgar Kelly, *Divine Providence in the England of Shakespeare's History Plays* (Cambridge, Mass.: Harvard University Press, 1970), and Wilbur Sanders, *The Dramatist and the Received Idea: Studies in the Plays of Marlowe and Shakespeare* (Cambridge: Cambridge University Press, 1968), offer different kinds of arguments against Tillyard's thesis about the roles of providential history and the Tudor myth in the histories. "New Historical" alternatives to Tillyard's approach may be sampled in Stephen Greenblatt's *Shakespearean Negotiations: The Circulation of Social Energy in Renaissance England* (Berkeley and Los Angeles: University of California Press, 1988) and in *Alternative Shakespeares*, ed. John Drakakis (London and New York: Methuen, 1985). For a sense of the "Tudor doctrine" emphasis when Tillyard's and Lily B. Campbell's studies were most influential, see Harold Jenkins, "Shakespeare's History Plays: 1900–1951," *ShS* 6 (1953): 1–15, and particularly his concluding remarks about "what can no longer be doubted." Dennis H. Burden updated Jenkins's survey in "Shakespeare's History Plays: 1952–1983," *ShS* 38 (1985): 1–18.

11. David Scott Kastan, "The Shape of Time: Form and Value in the Shakespearean History Play," *CompD* 7 (1982–83): 259–277, and *Shakespeare and the Shapes of Time* (Hanover: University Press of New England, 1982).

12. I use the terms *series* and *tetralogy* throughout to refer to the completed set and the two four-play groups of history plays, but with no assumption that the entire series or either tetralogy was preconceived as such. Likewise, my placement of *1 Henry VI* as first in the series involves no claim that it was written before Parts 2 and 3.

1. *1 Henry VI*

1. On the heroic style of this speech and the *Henry VI* trilogy, see James C. Bulman, *The Heroic Idiom of Shakespearean Tragedy* (Newark: University of Delaware Press; London and Toronto: Associated University Press, 1985), 26–50.

2. Any argument about this play and the *Henry VI* trilogy (or first tetralogy) must have constant reference to two fine studies: Edward I. Berry, *Patterns of Decay: Shakespeare's Early Histories* (Charlottesville: University Press of Virginia, 1975), and David Riggs, *Shakespeare's Heroical Histories: "Henry VI" and Its Literary Tradition* (Cambridge, Mass.: Harvard University Press, 1971). My major dis-

agreement with both, implicit in this last paragraph, may not be susceptible to absolute demonstration one way or the other. Both of them (Riggs with reference to the humanistic tradition of heroic achievement he traces through *Tamburlaine* to these plays) see the deterioration of England's polity through the trilogy as a matter of historical process that seems, as they describe it, to have a momentum carrying the characters along with it. Without denying the clear sense of progressive decay and its momentum, my argument posits the continued possibility of better or worse choices, particularly with respect to emulation of historic models and a positive regard for the past's relationship to the present. About the portrayed results, of course, there can be no disagreement, however the causes are interpreted and weighted.

3. David Kastan sees Talbot's death as signalling the failure of heroic exemplary history: *Shakespeare and the Shapes of Time* (Hanover: University Press of New England, 1982), 18–21. I accept Lucy's insistence on the failure of those who should support Talbot and live up to the ideal, rather than the failure of the ideal itself, as the play's primary emphasis here (IV, iii, 47–52).

4. For a more extended argument about the varying effects of soliloquies on an audience's point of view, see my *Engagement with Knavery: Point of View in "Richard III," "The Jew of Malta," "Volpone," and "The Revenger's Tragedy"* (Durham: Duke University Press, 1986), 10–11.

5. Thomas Nashe, *Pierce Penilesse His Supplication to the Divell*, in *The Works of Thomas Nashe*, ed. McKerrow, 1: 212.

6. On the characteristic inconclusiveness of the histories, see David Scott Kastan, "The Shapes of Time: Form and Value in the Shakespearean History Play," *CompD* 7 (1973–74): 259–277, and Kastan, *Shakespeare and the Shapes of Time*. Among the histories, however, *1 Henry VI*'s inconclusive ending is especially notable.

7. Here my view is clearly at odds with Berry's "inexorable law" of disintegration (*Patterns of Decay*, 52) and Riggs on "the dramatist's continuing discovery of an historical process that followed naturally from the extension of heroic ideals into Tudor politics" (*Shakespeare's Heroical Histories*, 129), although these particular phrases are applied to Parts 2 and 3. And my understanding of Talbot is much more in the spirit of Nashe than of John W. Blanpied, *Time and the Artist in Shakespeare's English Histories* (Newark: University of Delaware Press, 1983). Blanpied has Talbot metatheatrically exposed through the very flatness of his characterization as "the kind of hero you can only celebrate *in memoriam*" and "something of an embarrassment" onstage (29).

8. My phrasing here leaves out of account the degree to which lineage, or parentage, figured in the traditional idea of heroic renewal on which Shakespeare drew. See Riggs, *Shakespeare's Heroical Histories*, 24, 27, 62–92. Sigurd Burckhardt argues that Talbot and Shakespeare reach beyond the play's customary ceremonial style in the scene with the countess toward a more viable kind of style and

action: "'I Am But Shadow of Myself'": Ceremony and Design in *1 Henry VI*," *MLQ* 28 (1967): 139–158. James A. Ridell, in "Talbot and the Countess of Auvergne," *SQ* 28 (1977): 51–57, "corrects" Burckhardt, but in a way that ignores the more interesting reach of Burckhardt's argument.

2. *2 and 3 Henry VI*

1. Though I feel compelled here to register my personal reservations about the distinction in kind between Clifford's bloody revenge and Talbot's "bloody massacre" (*1HVI*, II, ii, 18), the plays surely intend the distinction between such personal revenge and battle against the national enemy to be clear and certain, even when Talbot speaks of "revenge" in the latter case (11). Berry notes Clifford's echoes and violations of Talbot's model as signals of the "new world" emerging at the end of 2 *Henry VI* (*Patterns of Decay*, 50–51). I would reserve the term *new world*, suggesting a fundamental change in the condition of things, for *Richard II*, where it is used in the play (IV, i, 78), and would speak here rather of deterioration which is not ultimately incurable or irreversible.

2. Margaret's lament for "former golden days" now lost refers to the sorry turn in her personal fortunes, not to a past when things were generally better, as Gaunt's and York's laments in *Richard II* will do.

3. *Richard III*

1. In his emphasis on the dominance of the past and the reassertion of continuity "in negative terms," though not in other respects, Edward Berry's discussion of *Richard III* in *Patterns of Decay* approximates mine here.

2. Consciousnesses on the rise have attended more in recent years to the roles allotted to women here and in the other histories (for example, Madonne M. Miner, "'Neither Mother, Wife, nor England's Queen': The Roles of Women in *Richard III*," in *The Woman's Part: Feminist Criticism of Shakespeare*, ed. Carolyn Ruth Swift Lenz, Gayle Greene, and Carol Thomas Neely [Urbana: University of Illinois Press, 1980], 35–55, and Phyllis Rackin, "Anti-Historians: Women's Roles in Shakespeare's Histories," *TJ* 37 [1985]: 329–344), and, to a lesser extent, to the aged (Terrance Brody Kearns, "'Brief Abstract and Record of Tedious Days': The Aged in *Richard III*," *PAPA* 13 [1987]: 25–34).

3. Nicholas Brooke argues that Richard's vital energy counters the inexorable and reductive force of the fixed moral order in the play: "Reflecting Gems and Dead Bones: Tragedy versus History in *Richard III*," *CritQ* 7 (1965): 123–134.

4. A. P. Rossiter led the way here, and no one could now speak, as he did, of theatrical talent as "an aspect of Richard's appeal which has . . . passed relatively unexamined": in *Angel with Horns*, ed. Storey, 16.

5. For a more extended analysis of Richard's "deft knavery," see my *Engagement with Knavery*, 27–62.

6. Richard's "triumph" here is a perplexing moment in the play, since if, as we may infer from the aftermath, Elizabeth is only pretending to give in, her lines give us none of the customary signals for such duplicity.

7. Richard was *not* "by" at the time of Henry's prophecy in *3 Henry VI* (IV, ii, 65–76).

8. David Kastan remarks that "Richmond is allowed to arrive unsullied by history" to play his role here: "'To Set a Form,'" 7.

9. Riggs, on the contrary, sees Richard's murder of Prince Edward as fatal to the humanistic heroic ideal voiced by the latter: *Shakespeare's Heroical Histories*, 150–151.

10. This whole paragraph contradicts Blanpied's thesis about the first tetralogy in *Time and the Artist*, and, with regard to Richmond, counters (among others) Judith H. Anderson, *Biographical Truth: The Representation of Historical Persons in Tudor-Stuart Writing* (New Haven: Yale University Press, 1984), 122–123. My point, of course, is not that Richmond (or any of the first tetralogy's other heroes) is "realistically" represented but that the presentation does not expose or subvert him as fictive with reference to an identifiably "truer" norm. As I suggested in my introduction, this way of seeing these heroes and these plays has the virtue of allowing what I believe to be significant distinctions in this regard between them and the histories that follow.

4. *King John*

1. See, for example, Virginia Mason Vaughan, "Between Tetralogies: *King John* as Transition," *SQ* 35 (1984): 407–420. On the play's tougher realism that counters simple moral history, see Sigurd Burckhardt, "*King John*: The Ordering of This Present Time," *ELH* 33 (1966): 133–153, and Eamon Grennan, "Shakespeare's Satirical History: A Reading of *King John*," *ShakS* 11 (1978): 21–37.

2. William H. Matchett, "Richard's Divided Heritage in *King John*," *EIC* 12 (1962): 234.

3. Falstaff is, of course, the other major fictive presence in the histories, and as irreverent commentators on the true events they observe, the Bastard and Falstaff share some important traits. But if Falstaff often takes the center of Shakespeare's stage, he is never allowed a central place in England's affairs. This crucial difference can be measured by trying to imagine Henry IV saying to Falstaff at Shrewsbury, as John says to the Bastard in V, i, "Have thou the ordering of this present time" (77). I should note that the source question is irrelevant to my argument here. My concern is with Shakespeare's use of this fictive character, whether he invented the Bastard himself or (as I suppose) refashioned him from *The Troublesome Raigne of John King of England*.

4. For a fuller argument focusing on the issues of "truth" and "right" in the play, see my "Truth in *King John*," *SEL* 23 (1985): 397–417.

5. My account of the Bastard may seem to ignore "flaws" in his character pointed out by those who would deny him full claim to the title of hero in John's play. The case against the Bastard is argued most strenuously by Julia C. Van de Water, "The Bastard in *King John*," *SQ* 11 (1960): 137–146. Ronald Stroud defends him with equal vigor in "The Bastard to the Time in *King John*," *CompD* 6 (1972): 154–166. Those who question the Bastard's character tend to do so through "objective" ethical scrutiny, whereas those who stress theatrical effect tend to put positive emphasis on his "special relationship with the audience," as does Emrys Jones, *The Origins of Shakespeare* (Oxford: Clarendon Press, 1977), 247.

6. This line proves to be an exclamation of disgust, not a preview of changing behavior. The Bastard's one subsequent assertion that "gold and silver becks" him on suggests, in its context, his eagerness to "shake" revenue for John out of "the bags / Of hoarding abbots" (III, iii, 6–13), and he continues to be John's (or England's) loyal subject.

7. Michael Manheim also notes this telling contrast between John's "terribly human" evil and Richard's more theatrical brand: *The Weak King Dilemma in the Shakespearean History Play* (Syracuse: Syracuse University Press, 1973), 133–135.

8. On the sense of history's indeterminacy in these plays, see John Wilders, *The Lost Garden: A View of Shakespeare's English and Roman History Plays* (London: Macmillan, 1978), 85–87, 94, 99. I would emphasize more than Wilders does the emergence of this sense in *John* and the second tetralogy.

9. Pandulph regains apparent control *offstage* after Lewis's unforeseen disaster, but our last theatrical views of both these political opportunists show them in postures of frustration as their plans go awry.

10. The motives of the nobles are rigorously questioned by James L. Calderwood, who accuses them of being hypocritical creatures of commodity: "Commodity and Honour in *King John*," *UTQ* 29 (1960): 341–356. I am not sure which view of the nobles, Calderwood's or mine, is more damaging to the prospects for a "true" solution to the problems this play exposes, but accepting his reading would not alter my essential thesis here.

11. Though I use the term *existential* here for want of a better one to describe the Bastard's choice of a course for which he knows no ultimate sanction is available, I do *not* mean to make him more of a philosopher than he actually is. Other readers place lines of reasoning in Richard's head here to make him a conventional Tudor homilist (Tillyard, *Shakespeare's History Plays*, 223–226) or a political New Man (Manheim, *The Weak King Dilemma*, 152–159). The Bastard does not explain his reasoning here, and I do not think he can—which is the point.

12. What follows here about the Bastard's "creative" effort is partly anticipated by Kastan, "'To Set a Form,'" 1–16.

13. Kastan points out how the "fictions of stability" supporting kingship are exposed in the first tetralogy (ibid., 4–7), and such a sequence as Henry VI's

fantasy-flight into the world of pastoral in *3 Henry VI*, II, iv, provides precedent for the sort of contrast between imagination's desires and reality's limits that Salisbury's speech evokes here. But (Blanpied to the contrary in *Time and the Artist*) the first tetralogy does not open the question of historical authenticity and historical fiction to the significant extent that *King John* does.

14. Others who have noted the Bastard's heroic heritage from Cordelion along with Matchett ("Richard's Divided Heritage") include John F. Danby, *Shakespeare's Doctrine of Nature* (London: Faber and Faber, 1949), 77; Robert B. Pierce, *Shakespeare's History Plays: The Family and the State* (Columbus: Ohio State University Press, 1971), 139; and Jones, *Origins*, 247.

15. On the Bastard's fictive status and likely derivation from various sources, see Peter Saccio, *Shakespeare's English Kings: History, Chronicle, and Drama* (New York: Oxford University Press, 1977), 205.

16. Among those who credit the Bastard for declining the crown are Irving Ribner, who edits and introduces the play in *The Complete Pelican Shakespeare*, ed. Alfred Harbage (Baltimore: Penguin Books, 1969), 601, and Calderwood, "Commodity and Honour," 356. William Matchett argues that our historical knowledge does not prevent Shakespeare from using structure to surprise us at the end with Prince Henry's sudden appearance, and I can agree with him to this extent. But for Matchett, "the question is, will . . . [the Bastard], like John, usurp the throne" when the opportunity presents itself in Act V ("Richard's Divided Heritage," 251–253). Once that question actually arises for us, consciousness of the fictive Bastard's inability to do any such thing must follow and must thereby modify our understanding of the exemplary behavior for which Matchett and others praise him.

17. I am happy to borrow Kastan's useful phrase here and elsewhere.

5. *Richard II*

1. Studies that emphasize the idea of the Fall in this play include those of Stanley R. Maveety, "A Second Fall of Cursed Man: The Bold Metaphor in *Richard II*," *JEGP* 72 (1973): 175–193, and Clayton G. MacKenzie, "Paradise and Paradise Lost in *Richard II*," *SQ* 37 (1986): 318–339. John Wilders, *The Lost Garden: A View of Shakespeare's English and Roman History Plays* (London: Macmillan, 1978), does not give *Richard II* special attention for using the Fall as a model for an ideal past—a model he presents as common to the histories, which he tends to treat as of a kind with the tragedies in this regard.

2. For a stringent antidote to my essentially benign (if not altogether credulous) reading of Gaunt's remembrance of a better England, see Donald M. Friedman, who sees the self-interested war lord showing through the guardian of values: "John of Gaunt and the Rhetoric of Frustration," *ELH* 43 (1976): 279–299.

3. One might recall (and Shakespeare may have recalled) in this regard Cas-

tiglione on old men's characteristic praise of their past and blame of the present at the beginning of Book Two of *The Book of the Courtier.*

4. York's formulaic phrasing may be placed in the context of studies that focus on outmoded language and its failures in this play and in the entire second tetralogy. See Joan Webber, "The Renewal of the King's Symbolic Role: From *Richard II* to *Henry V*," *TSLL* 4 (1963): 530–538; Anne Barton, "Shakespeare and the Limitations of Language," *ShS* 24 (1971): 19–30; James L. Calderwood, *Metadrama in Shakespeare's Henriad: "Richard II" to "Henry V"* (Berkeley and Los Angeles: University of California Press, 1979); Joseph A. Porter, *The Drama of Speech Acts: Shakespeare's Lancastrian Tetralogy* (Berkeley: University of California Press, 1979); and Ronald R. MacDonald, "Uneasy Lies: Language and History in Shakespeare's Lancastrian Tetralogy," *SQ* 35 (1984): 22–39.

5. John Blanpied maintains that Richard's deviation from "the ideal model (his grandfather, Edward III)" is part of his self-conscious performance of the role of king: *Time and the Artist,* 122. Richard often *does* "perform," of course, but I see nothing studied in his negligence of the past or in his evident incomprehension of York's concern in this regard.

6. For a general account of father-son relationships and their significance in this play and the other histories, see Robert B. Pierce, *Shakespeare's History Plays: The Family and the State* (Columbus: Ohio State University Press, 1971).

7. See note 4 above on the elders' outmoded language. The question of the past's fictive status would also complicate the views of historical eras in the play posited by Tillyard, *Shakespeare's History Plays*; Peter G. Philias, "The Medieval in *Richard II*," *SQ* 12 (1961): 305–310; and Robert Hapgood, "Three Eras in *Richard II*," *SQ* 14 (1963): 281–283. One could cite Peter Ure's note in his New Arden edition of the play (Cambridge, Mass.: Harvard University Press, 1956) on York's questionable recollection of saving the Black Prince (II, iii, 98–104) as evidence that the old duke fabricates his memories; but, as with some other recollections that clash with Shakespeare's available sources, there is no tip-off in the play that this one is faulty.

8. York's formula nicely "revives" the double thrust of the Black Prince's own order for the effigy on his tomb, which was to show him "fully armed in the pride of battle . . . our face meek and our leopard helm placed beneath our head": cited from a variety of sources by Barbara W. Tuchman, *A Distant Mirror: The Calamitous 14th Century* (New York: Alfred A. Knopf, 1978), 294. Compare Henry V's prescription in *Henry V*, III, i, 3–6:

> In peace there's nothing so becomes a man
> As modest stillness and humility,
> But when the blast of war blows in our ears,
> Then imitate the action of the tiger.

9. Of the many accounts of the play's ambivalence about the experience it dramatizes, I would refer a reader first of all to Norman Rabkin, *Shakespeare and*

the Common Understanding (New York: Free Press; London: Collier-Macmillan, 1967), 81–95.

6. *1 Henry IV*

1. Of the analyses of Hal's success where others fail, Harold Toliver's may most closely approximate mine: "Workable Fictions in the *Henry IV* Plays," *UTQ* 53 (1983–84): 53–71. Alvin B. Kernan offers an excellent overview of the tetralogy in this regard in "The Henriad: Shakespeare's Major History Plays," in *Modern Shakespearean Criticism: Essays on Style, Dramaturgy, and the Major Plays*, ed. Alvin B. Kernan (New York: Harcourt, Brace and World, 1970), 245–275. Like Derek Traversi's more extended argument in *Shakespeare from "Richard II" to "Henry V"* (London: Hollis and Carter; Palo Alto: Stanford University Press, 1957), and like several other studies, Kernan's essay emphasizes a changing world to which Hal responds successfully, and all such arguments therefore suggest a historical process portrayed through the plays in which older ways fail in the face of new conditions. With their focus on the uses of language, outmoded and otherwise, the works cited in Chapter 5, note 5, are also concerned with this process. My more particular concern here is with the varying views of the past and its relationship to the present voiced by characters in the plays and with our perspective on those views.

2. Riggs notes that Hal "stands outside the paradigm of example and emulation" and remakes "the heroic tradition . . . in his own image": *Shakespeare's Heroical Histories*, 160. For Traversi, Hal "represents rather a fresh beginning than a continuation": *Shakespeare from "Richard II" to "Henry V,"* 3.

3. Edward Berry emphasizes the way in which history becomes "internalized, . . . nearly swallowed up by the subjective dimension of personal memory" in the second tetralogy: *Patterns of Decay*, 111. Bernard McElroy offered an instructive analysis of reconstructive retrospection in the second tetralogy in "Drawing Anew the Model: The Invention of the Past in Shakespeare's Historical Dramas," a paper presented at the Ohio Shakespeare Conference, March 1, 1986, at the Ohio State University.

4. James L. Calderwood shows in detail how Hal validates his "truth" with reference to Falstaff's fictions: *Metadrama in Shakespeare's Henriad: "Richard II" to "Henry V"* (Berkeley and Los Angeles: University of California Press, 1979), chaps. 3 and 4.

5. Again, I only adumbrate what has been pointed out elsewhere about Hotspur's "old" ways in a new world. See Anthony La Branche, "'If Thou Wert Sensible of Courtesy': Private and Public Virtue in *Henry IV, Part One*," *SQ* 17 (1966): 371–382; and, on the public and private values that jar in Hal's success through the *Henriad*, Julian Markels, *The Pillar of the World: "Antony and Cleopatra" in Shakespeare's Development* (Columbus: Ohio State University Press, 1968), 51–77.

6. On Hal's "absorption" of Hotspur's heroic identity, see Harold Toliver, "Falstaff, the Prince, and the History Play," *SQ* 16 (1965): 71, and Derek Cohen, "The Rite of Violence in *1 Henry IV*," *ShS* 38 (1985): 77–84.

7. *2 Henry IV*

1. John Wilders generalizes about this impulse to turn *both* ways from the present in the histories: *The Lost Garden*, 9–10, 125–126.

2. I would disagree here with at least the wording of Ronald R. MacDonald, who sees "much more than a tinge" of Henry's Part One nostalgia in these Part Two memories: "Uneasy Lies: Language and History in Shakespeare's Lancastrian Tetralogy," *SQ* 35 (1984): 36. If *this* is nostalgia, then the graffiti in my department's men's room is right, and "nostalgia isn't what it used to be."

3. The exception to this relegation of classical models to the "subplot"—references to Caesar and Priam in the opening scene—will be noted shortly.

4. Warwick's own actual expectations of Henry V, revealed at the beginning of V, ii, are right in line with his pragmatic (and faulty) theory of historically based prognoses and therefore belie his consolation of the king in IV, iv, 67–78. Ricardo J. Quinones cites and comments on Guicciardini's comparable reflections in *Ricordi* on the indeterminacy of historical examples as guides to the future ("58. How wisely the philosopher spoke when he said: 'Of future contingencies there can be no determined truth.' . . . 117. To judge by example can be very misleading"): *The Renaissance Discovery of Time* (Cambridge, Mass.: Harvard University Press, 1972), 184.

5. Harry Berger, Jr., analyzes the unsettling effects of Rumor's Induction in "Sneak's Noise or Rumor and Detextualization," *KR* n.s. 6 (1984): 58–78.

6. Berger, who remarks on the guilt that freights Northumberland's nihilism ("Sneak's Noise," 68–72), credits G. R. Hibbard for noting the anticipation of Lear and Macbeth here in *The Making of Shakespeare's Dramatic Poetry* (Toronto: Toronto University Press, 1981), 170–171.

7. For an account of Talbot's death less adulatory than Lucy's (and less jaundiced than Joan's), see Tuchman, *A Distant Mirror*, 593–594.

8. It should be noted that Henry's disillusionment in III, i, is not based on the kind of complete vision he imagines, since he mistakes Hal's past, present, and future; but his discouraged focus here is on his own career as it appeared "then" and appears "now."

8. *Henry V*

1. Readers arguing ironic subversion of the hero king find dark notes in the appeal to the Black Prince. See Roy W. Battenhouse, "*Henry V* as Heroic

Comedy," in *Essays on Shakespeare and Elizabethan Drama in Honor of Hardin Craig*, ed. Richard Hosley (Columbia: University of Missouri Press, 1962), 174.

2. Ironic readings may be represented by Harold C. Goddard, *The Meaning of Shakespeare* (Chicago: University of Chicago Press, 1951), 215–268, and, in a more learned academic vein, by Battenhouse, "*Henry V* as Heroic Comedy." The opposite extreme can be found in John Dover Wilson's introduction to his New Cambridge edition (Cambridge: Cambridge University Press, 1947). More recent readings tend away from these "either/or" extremes toward "both/and" complexity. For a fine example of the latter, insisting on both extremes rather than a comfortable compromise, see Norman Rabkin, *Shakespeare and the Problem of Meaning* (Chicago: University of Chicago Press, 1982), 33–62. And though our approaches differ, I agree with Stephen Greenblatt's account of the audience's participatory overcoming of Henry's perceived "imperfections" in *Shakespearean Negotiations: The Circulation of Social Energy in Renaissance England* (Berkeley and Los Angeles: University of California Press, 1988), 62–64.

3. Edward I. Berry also uses *Edward III* as a comparative foil, though with a different focus and a different point in mind: "'True Things and Mock'ries': Epic and History in *Henry V*," *JEGP* 78 (1979): 1–16. I quote the Black Prince's speech from *The Raigne of King Edward the Third* in *The Shakespeare Apocrypha*, ed. C. F. Tucker Brooke (Oxford: Clarendon Press, 1918), 101.

4. For a fuller explication of Henry as a shaper of history and collaborator with the chorus, see Eamon Grennan, "'This Story Shall the Good Man Teach His Son': *Henry V* and the Art of History," *PLL* 15 (1979): 370–382. Henry's speech to his soldiers is, of course, an exhortation suited to the occasion, not an essay on historiography. But compare the Black Prince's inspirational speech in similar circumstances in *Edward III*, IV, iv, 40–65, which rhetorically "transforms" the mighty French force in terms customary to such occasions (the "they put their pants on one leg at a time just like we do" line) without showing any of Henry's self-consciousness about shaping both the occasion and future reports of it.

5. Rabkin, *Shakespeare and the Problem of Meaning*, 34–35.

6. This awareness that he cannot determine events shows through his way of posing alternatives dependent on their outcome. See, for example, I, iii, 226–234 and IV, iii, 20–22. For a fine reading of the night scene encounter with Williams which finds Shakespeare's "fundamentally tragic" conception of history in it rather than any simple ironic subversion, see Anne Barton, "The King Disguised: Shakespeare's *Henry V* and the Comical History," in *The Triple Bond: Plays, Mainly Shakespearean, in Performance*, ed. Joseph G. Price (University Park and London: Pennsylvania State University Press, 1975), 92–117.

7. Richard Levin, *New Readings vs. Old Plays* (Chicago: University of Chicago Press, 1979), 97–98, 209–229.

8. David Quint reviews Alexander's status as an exemplary figure before Fluellen's use and abuse of him as such: "'Alexander the Pig': Shakespeare on History and Poetry," *Boundary* 10 (1982): 49–68. Robert P. Merrix takes a learned route

to satiric irony in "The Alexandrian Allusion in *Henry V*," *ELR* 2 (1972): 321–333.

9. For a fine appreciation of Orson Welles's evocation of this poignancy in *The Chimes at Midnight*, see Samuel Crowl, "The Long Goodbye: Welles and Falstaff," *SQ* 31 (1980): 369–380.

10. See Alfred Harbage's note on II, Chorus, 41 in his edition of the play in *The Complete Pelican Shakespeare*.

11. Treatments of the Chorus, of course, help to determine (or are determined by) ironic and celebrative readings of the play. For a good review of the subject, see Lawrence Danson, "*Henry V*: King, Chorus, and Critics," *SQ* 34 (1983): 27–43. Other readings that approximate and supplement mine in this regard include those of Peter B. Erickson, "'The Fault / My Father Made': The Anxious Pursuit of Heroic Fame in Shakespeare's *Henry V*," *MLS* 10 (1979–80): 10–25, and Edward I. Berry, "'True Things and Mock'ries': Epic and History in *Henry V*," *JEGP* 78 (1979): 1–16.

12. *Samuel Johnson on Shakespeare*, ed. William K. Wimsatt, Jr. (New York: Hill and Wang, 1960), 92, 38–40. Cited by Erickson, "'The Fault / My Father Made,'" 12.

13. Ibid.

14. For an energetic account of our participation, see Michael Goldman, *Shakespeare and the Energies of Drama* (Princeton: Princeton University Press, 1972), 58–73.

15. On the other hand, prophets in the plays who look ahead to events already past before Shakespeare's time have an obvious advantage over the Chorus and his hopes for Essex, which are subject to unconscious irony from our perspective, if not from the original audience's. On this general topic, see Marjorie Garber, "What's Past Is Prologue: Temporality and Prophecy in Shakespeare's History Plays," in *Renaissance Genres: Essays on Theory, History, and Interpretation*, ed. Barbara K. Lewalski (Cambridge, Mass.: Harvard University Press, 1986), 301–331. R. L. Smallwood comments on the "then/now" effect of *Henry V* and its chorus: "Shakespeare's Use of History," in *The Cambridge Companion to Shakespeare Studies*, ed. Stanley Wells (Cambridge: Cambridge University Press, 1986), 143–144. And Paul Ricoeur's discussion of the historian's "temporal perspectives" is of special interest here, though there are ways in which his posited "projection into another present, which belongs to the type of objectivity proper to history," differs from Shakespeare's: *History and Truth* (Evanston: Northwestern University Press, 1965), 28.

16. Goddard, *Meaning of Shakespeare*, 218.

17. Edward Berry, distinguishing between the heroical and historical modes here, refers appropriately to Sidney's *Apologie for Poetrie*: "'True Things and Mock'ries,'" 2–4.

18. The double referent of the Chorus's "small time" has been noted by Joseph

A. Porter, *The Drama of Speech Acts: Shakespeare's Lancastrian Tetralogy* (Berkeley: University of California Press, 1979), 185, and by James L. Calderwood, *Metadrama in Shakespeare's Henriad: "Richard II" to "Henry V"* (Berkeley and Los Angeles: University of California Press, 1979), 160–161. Both books focus on the use of language and on ways in which Hal/Henry's use of it enables him; and both (especially Calderwood's), though with this different focus and interest, approximate my account of the prince and his career.

INDEX

Anderson, Judith H., 159n.10

Bacon, Francis, xii, xiii
Barton, Anne, 162n.4, 165n.6
Battenhouse, Roy W., 164n.1,
    165n.2
Berger, Harry, Jr., 164n.5, 164n.6
Berners, Lord (Sir John Bourchier), xi
Berry, Edward I., 156n.2, 157n.7,
    158n.1, 163n.3, 165n.3, 166n.11,
    166n.17
Black Prince, viii, 20, 29, 32, 70, 76,
    77, 80, 81–82, 89, 93, 127, 129,
    130, 131, 134, 136, 140, 164n.1,
    165n.3, 165n.4
Blanpied, John W., 156n.9, 157n.7,
    159n.10, 161n.13, 162n.5
Brooke, Nicholas, 158n.3
Browning, Robert, viii
Bulman, James C., 156n.1
Burckhardt, Sigurd, 157n.8, 159n.1
Burden, Dennis H., 156n.10

Calderwood, James L., 160n.10,
    161n.16, 162n.4, 163n.4, 168n.18
Campbell, Lily B., 156n.10
Castiglione, Baldassare: *The Book of the
    Courtier*, 161n.3
Chaucer, Geoffrey: *The Legend of Good
    Women*, 105
Chorus: role of, in *Henry V.*, 130–
    131, 133, 135, 144–145, 146–
    154, 166n.15
Cohen, Derek, 164n.6
Crowl, Samuel, 166n.9

Danby, John F., 161n.14
Danson, Lawrence, 166n.11

Edward III, 129, 138, 165n.3,
    165n.4
Erickson, Peter B., 166n.11, 166n.12,
    166n.13

Friedman, Donald M., 161n.2
Froissart, Jean, xi, xii, 155n.2
Fussner, F. Smith, 155n.5
Future: anticipations of, 96, 97–99,
    101, 109, 112, 131–132; dread of,
    112; shaping of, in present, 99–
    103, 107–110, 116–117, 130–
    131

Garber, Marjorie, 166n.15
Goddard, Harold C., 151, 165n.2,
    166n.16
Goldman, Michael, 166n.14
Gombrich, E. H., 133
Greenblatt, Stephen, 156n.10,
    165n.2
Grennan, Eamon, 159n.1, 165n.4
Guicciardini: *Ricordi*, 164n.4

Hapgood, Robert, 162n.7
Harbage, Alfred, 166n.10
Hibbard, G. R., 164n.6
History: classical heroes from, 29, 43–
    44, 115–116, 128, 136–139; con-
    scious creation of, in present, 99–
    103, 107–110, 116–117, 130–
    133, 135, 145; constitutional and
    legal rights in relation to, 20–22,
    27, 48–52, 64, 75–79, 82–83,
    85–87; *de casibus* versions of, 7,
    90–91; as dramatically conceived
    by Shakespeare, xi, xiii, xiv, 10–14,
    16, 19–21, 28, 45, 47, 62–68,

DATE DUE
